The Philadelphia

ITALIAN MARKET

COOKBOOK

The Tastes of
South 9th Street

The Philadelphia

ITALIAN MARKET

COOKBOOK

The Tastes of South 9th Street

BY

CELESTE A. MORELLO

Cover design by Celeste A. Morello.
Graphic Design by Frank J. Szerbin.

Library of Congress Catalog Card Number: 99-096482.

ISBN 0-9677334-0-5

TABLE OF CONTENTS

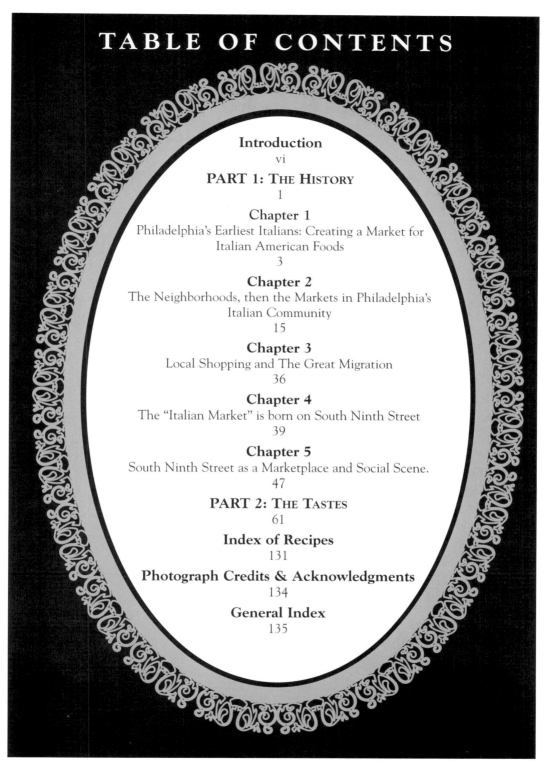

Introduction

My FAMILY'S BUSINESS will soon be entering its third century of providing Italian-style foods to Philadelphia and throughout the United States and world. The Marano family began importing products to Philadelphia's "Little Italy" community before there was a 9th Street Italian Market! You might say that my family's business was an emporium for Italian foods but without the camaraderie, noise and bargaining dialogue as in the open air markets.

My earliest recollections of walking through the Italian Market on 9th Street was with my father. He would take me into the butcher stores, the stores where oils, spices and other things were sold and outside of the stores where the live animals were in pens. It was a place where one could shop, second to none in Philadelphia, a true marketplace. I don't know if even New York has a 9th Street Market with which to compare!

I admire the merchants who are truly 9th Street because they work hard for their customers to continue a tradition of shopping in a place whose history has meaning for all of Philadelphia as well as those who visit.

LUKE MARANO, SR.
Chairman, Philadelphia Macaroni Company
Former Chairperson, National Pasta Assn. (NPA) and
1992 "Pasta Man of the Year"

ABBREVIATIONS

t = teaspoon

T = tablespoon

C = cup, or 8 ounces

lb. = pound, or 16 ounces

"pinch" = whatever quantity can be placed between the thumb and index finger. Individual tastes may vary.

"salt & pepper" = to any individual's own taste. These can also be omitted, depending on dietary needs.

Note to cooks who intend to use these recipes:

—Carefully read the recipes before trying them.

—You may want to substitute different types of cooking vessels for others, e.g., a Dutch oven for a deep frying pan.

—Use with whatever you are most comfortable.

—Give yourself enough time to prepare each recipe.

Welcome to the tastes

of the

ITALIAN MARKET!

PART 1

A. Liguria
B. Abruzzi
C. Campania
D. Calabria
E. Sicily

THE HISTORY

The map of Italy on the previous page shows emphasized regions for location.

CHAPTER

Philadelphia's Earliest Italians:
Creating a Market
for
Italian American Foods

Lᴏɴɢ BEFORE THERE WAS AN ITALIAN MARKET on South Ninth Street there were many groups of individuals living in various parts of Philadelphia who claimed Italian as their native language. Italy was not yet a country until 1860, but Italian-speakers from almost every section of the mainland and islands lived in Philadelphia and its outlying districts before and after the Revolution.[1]

It was not unusual nor a coincidence of history: Philadelphia was the second largest English-speaking city in the world and the most important city in the colonies just before the U.S. declared independence. In fact, our city continued to rival with London even well into the nineteenth century. And the influence of the land surrounding ancient Rome likewise was seen, heard and tasted in both English-speaking countries.

As a new nation, the U.S. had been accustomed to many of Italy's foods. Thomas Jefferson and Benjamin Franklin encouraged the importation of wines, cheeses and other edibles.[2] The Italy as we know of in 1999 was formerly a collection of lands ruled by Austria, the Bourbons and the oft-militant Popes in 1789. Then, Philadelphia was capitol of the U.S. and drew those from this peninsula more for enterprise than for opportunity and to escape poverty.

Dr. Richard N. Juliani of Villanova University, a scholar of Italian American studies for over thirty years documented Philadelphia's burgeoning "Little Italy" in the early nineteenth century and found an Italian-speaker, a sausage-maker who sold what was perhaps the first real Italian food in our city.[3] But he was not very successful, at least as a retailer in Italian food.

Together with other Italian-speaking individuals, the small population in Philadelphia drew more males from what is now Italy. But the group of Italian-speaking males could hardly be called a colony: the women usually did not migrate with their men. According to Juliani, there were few Italian-speaking women who were noted in the documentation apparently because they were not yet recognized as a work force. Juliani's analysis showed a rather accelerated acculturation of mostly males who were marrying native-born Americans or immigrants from Great Britain or northern Europe who were living in Philadelphia. Perhaps if more females from the Italian peninsula settled here, Italian food would have been common at an earlier date with these settlers. But it seemed as if the Italian-speaking men "converted" to their wives' ways in Philadelphia, meaning a diet without macaroni and tomato gravy.

These first men to speak Italian in Philadelphia were employed in skilled jobs such as musicians or teachers or sculptors[4] but rarely anything food-related until the arrival of the women or their families. Consequently, there was no demand for Italian food products with the rise of the new identification of the "Americanized" Italian-speaker. To be an American then was interpreted to mean a denial of Italian food.

It was not until about the 1840s when couples and families of Italian-speaking immigrants began to settle throughout Philadelphia, city and County.[5] They belonged to various Roman Catholic and non-Catholic denominations, although the former religion did well to organize this ethnic group primarily around the Italian language as the unifying element. No better prelate in Philadelphia understood the importance of language than Bishop John Neumann, an immigrant from Bohemia who realized that the church was as central to the new settlers as their language. Neumann experienced the village church as the foundation for a community in his native land, as it was throughout Christian Europe. He used this same concept in Philadelphia with the Italian-speakers by the early 1850s. In 1852, Neumann purchased a Methodist church and "colored graveyard" on

Marriott Street in Moyamensing Township (now part of South Philadelphia) and instituted the first Italian Catholic church in the United States.

It was a "national church" although no Italian nation existed until 1860.

The first pastor, the Reverend Gaetano Mariani named the church, "St. Mary Magdalen de Pazzi" after a Florentine Carmelite nun, although the congregation was largely from Liguria.

And, although there were other Italian-speakers from other regions on the peninsula, the only common bonds that these immigrants had were religion, language, similar experiences of then-living in Philadelphia, and, their interactions with the *'mericani.*

Ironies, Contradictions. And lots of excitement. It's a history that characterizes the food in the Italian Market!

St. Mary Magdalen de Pazzi's parish records indicate that most of their parishioners hailed from the northwestern section of modern Italy called, Liguria. The first settlers from this area around Genoa who would make their mark in the food industry in Philadelphia found their way to the area between South Street and Washington Avenue, from Sixth and Ninth Streets. John Raggio, from Romaggi, came to this neighborhood after briefly owning a macaroni factory in Boston. Raggio, as many other Ligurians, figured in the many produce huckster jobs which also kept the vendor well fed. Raggio's great-great grandson, Louis Arata said that his other Ligurian ancestors from Cicagni came to live within St. Mary Magdalen's parish in the 1860s, representing a group intent on joining fellow Ligurians who had broken new ground a generation before.

Louis Arata's recollection of his family's ties with food is filled with stories of his forebearers here pushing carts of produce and owning grocery stores during most of the 19th century. Because there was no "Italian" market in the 1880s and 1890s, Arata's grandparents had to hawk their produce at the Bainbridge Street Market. They were typical of the South Philadelphians whose native Italian tongue and rural lifestyle gradually americanized. By the time that Louis was born in 1931, not much of his Ligurian heritage was left on U.S. soil. But, "Oh, my grandmother's ravioli!" An extraordinary dish, this ravioli was a stuffing of greens and veal and seasonings, enrobed in a delicate dough that floated in a thin tomato sauce. It was a favorite of the Arata family.

Over the years, Louis and his wife, Mary Costa Arata embarked on personal history journeys which went beyond their 19th century Italian Market neighborhood roots to their ancestral homes near Genoa. There, "The mountains go down to the coast and terrace the hillside [which mean] more land to till," said Louis, who walked in the steps of the men and women who left their Ligurian villages for an American city. While in the hamlet of Chiavari, Louis and Mary sampled classic Ligurian foods such as farinata, pesto sauce in a variety of dishes and lots of seafood that reflect the short distance between the mountains and coastal area. Louis and Mary, whose family lived high up in Sopralacroce, near Chiavari, said that very little, if any variation existed in the cooking style of the lowlands. The area's hearty weather makes for produce, dairy and seafood to blend into tastes that distinguish this cuisine from other types of regional cooking.

As for macaroni, the tomato sauce was, "extremely thin, almost watery," said Mary. Nevertheless, a thin sauce is what is recommended with this ravioli recipe which is really what the Genovese use. The following recipe has been simplified but, said Louis and Mary, their grandmothers used the traditional meat, that is, calves' brains, with or without veal with the greens. However, if one does choose to use the calves' brains, note the changes in the recipe:

LIGURIAN-STYLE RAVIOLI

Filling:

1 lb.	spinach that has already been washed and dried and cut into pieces
1/2 lb.	ground veal (or 1/4 lb. if using 1/4 lb. calves' brains)

3 T	olive oil	2 T	parsley flakes
2	eggs, beaten	2 oz.	any grated cheese
1	medium onion, diced		salt and salt and pepper to taste

Dough: See page 7.

Precook the greens and set aside. In a skillet, saute the onion until golden, then add the veal and cook until done. In a bowl, place the cooled meat with the greens and blend in the eggs, cheese, salt and pepper to consistency.

In Italian homes, the "cooks" usually use a dessert glass, (or large lipped thick glass) to make ravioli. Roll out the dough into a thin sheet and judge, by the size of the diameter of the glass, how many 2-sided ravioli can be cut from the sheet. Spoon the mixture onto the dough about 2" apart in a long row. Make sure that there is enough dough to fold over to cover the filling. Fold dough over to cover, "cut" with the glass and seal each ravioli by pressing down with the tips of a fork.

Boil the ravioli in salted water until the dough is cooked. The Aratas as Genovese, said that their ravioli is almost palm-sized. Figure about 3 to 4 ravioli per serving or more. This recipe can provide fillings for about 16 ravioli (or about 4 servings.)

Here is one of Mary Costa Arata's favorite Ligurian dishes which have been adapted:

MUSSELS GENOVESE

2 doz. mussels, debearded and cleaned

2 qts. prepared marinara sauce   basil to taste

2 T   olive oil   salt & pepper to taste

1 C   heavy cream

In a deep (6") pot, warm the marinara sauce over medium heat. Add water to thin the sauce and put in mussels. Cover to steam until mussels are opened. Uncover. Let mussels and sauce cool, remove shells from pot and skim off bits of tomato. Add cream to thinned tomato sauce. Taste for seasoning, mix and serve alone or over any macaroni.

The Ligurians, like others from the Italian peninsula, found that the most convenient food which they could easily make in Philadelphia, as they had done at home, was pasta. The same flour used for bread was used to make home-made macaroni if one did not buy the imported brands in the 1850s here. One local Philadelphia newspaperman may have unknowingly cornered the city's largest Italian-speaking colony's culinary roots in 1852 when he wrote: "Italy abounds in Macaroni and Vermicelli...into all their soups and pastry, and into many meat dishes."[6] Actually, some of the immigrants may have been making their own macaroni until later when factories that specialized in "maccaroni" arose. But before these businesses, the newspaperman cited, "Genoa, from which place I think we get most of our Macaroni...Here it is nearer the color of bread."[7] It depends. This basic dough to make macaroni calls for white flour, is rather simple and very flexible to use.

MACARONI DOUGH

(For 4 to 5 adult servings)

Use one cup of flour per adult   salt (optional)

2 or 3 eggs   water on side (at room temp.)

On a clean table or large board, put five cups of flour into a mound. With your hand, partially "hollow out" the center of the flour, but do not clear the bottom of the mound. Break the eggs into the mound and work in the flour, slowly adding the water to form a soft dough. Add more water if the dough is too dry or more flour if the dough is too wet. The dough should be soft and pliable. Form a single ball of dough and put on the board or table to prepare for kneading. Roll out the dough with a rolling pin until the dough is about 1/8" thick. For the ravioli, roll the dough thinner.

To make fettuccini-like macaroni:

Roll out dough to thin sheet on a floured surface. When dough sheet is even in thickness, slowly roll into a cylinder. Make horizontal cuts into this cylindrical roll. These cuts should be to one's choice: 1/4" or 1/2" in width. Break these strips off and let lay on the floured surface to dry or to prepare to boil in salted water.

This dough can also be used in a macaroni/pasta machine for more varied cuts.

Two of the earliest makers of macaroni and pasta products in Philadelphia's growing "Little Italy" were Cuneo & Lagomarsino's at Eighth and Christian Streets and Guano and Raggio's, later, "The American Macaroni Company" at Seventh and Montrose Streets. True to their Ligurian culinary tradition, there were many ravioli with spinach fillings manufactured and sold within St. Mary Magdalen's parish. Other ravioli fillings used in the Genoa area which were duplicated in the immigrant colony included an egg and spinach mix, seasoned sausage removed from its casing and other green vegetables combined with bitter greens.

Other descendants from these Ligurians in Philadelphia have contributed family recipes.

Bennedetta Gandolfo Donato (1878-1948) passed on her "Railroad Cake" to her daughter who gave it to Michael DiPilla. "It's supposed to be brown and plain like a railroad car," she explained. It typified the simple fare of the first immigrants from northern Italy who settled in Philadelphia.

Cuneo & Lagomarsino's "Maccaroni Works" at 8th & Christian Streets. c. 1909.

BENNEDETTA GANDOLFO DONATO'S RAILROAD CAKE

1 C	sugar	1 t	baking powder
4 T	melted butter	1 t	vanilla
2	eggs, beaten	1/2 C	milk
1 1/2 C flour			

"Put it all together and beat by hand for five minutes. Grease and flour a small loaf-shaped pan and bake at 325°F for 25 minutes."

If this cake is not already sweet enough and too plain, sprinkle with 10X sugar or ice with bitter sweet chocolate.

❦

Bishop James Schad, retired auxiliary Bishop of Camden is the grandson of Benedicta Columba Cuneo and Giacomo Gandolfo. Born in 1917, the bishop grew up on Ligurian cuisine, the legacy of his beloved mother. The bishop explained these dishes to me and I followed with these interpretations.

"SKIRT STEAK"

4	(4 oz.) steaks, 1/2" thick, pounded	1	(16 oz.) can, spinach, with water
1/2 C	Italian seasoned bread crumbs	1/3 C locatelli, grated	
1	egg	pepper to taste	

Lay the pounded steaks flat and season with salt and pepper, if desired. In a bowl, combine the spinach, egg, breadcrumbs, and cheese and then fill each steak sheet with about 1/2 C of the stuffing. Tie each with a cooking twine to make four stuffed bundles. Bake in an oven on 350°F occasionally turning the bundles until the entire steak is done.

Bishop Schad said that this is served without sauce and that the spinach's water should keep the meat moist.

BISHOP SCHAD'S MOTHER'S RISOTTO GENOVESE

2 C	white rice	1/2 C	(or more) fresh leaf basil, chopped
1/4 C	locatelli, grated	1/2 C	(or more) sweet red pepper, chopped
4 T tomato sauce			

Boil the rice as directed. Drain and set the hot rice aside. In a sauté pan, steam the red pepper with the basil until they are cooked. Combine these with the rice, then stir in the tomato sauce. Before serving, toss the rice with locatelli cheese.

Serves about 4.

And, of course, pesto!

PESTO SAUCE

This is the traditional recipe.

2 C	basil	2	cloves, garlic, diced
1/4 C	pinuola nuts	1 C	olive oil
1/2 C	any good grating cheese combination (e.g., parmesan & locatelli) or just parmesan		salt (opt.)
warm water or heavy cream			fresh ground black pepper (opt.)

This is one of those flexible recipes that can be adjusted to increase the amount of cheese, basil and oil, or decrease any of the ingredients to suit one's taste.

Mix all of the ingredients together to form a smooth consistency. Add more of the liquids for a thinner sauce; more basil and cheese for a thicker blend.

In time, almost anyone in Philadelphia who was foreign and who spoke Italian gravitated towards St. Mary Magdalen's Church. Soon, rowhouses would be built around the church. Work however, was outside of the growing colony as was the food. Produce and meats were purchased in Center City or near the docks. The closest market was the shed on Bainbridge Street. Then the South Eleventh Street Market arose but not for any ethnic group's needs. If any of St. Mary Magdalen's early parishioners were involved in foodstuffs, it was still outside of the immigrant colony with only a few exceptions. Lorenzo Arata, who lived across from St. Mary Magdalen's sold the produce that he purchased from the port in Center City where the traffic was greater than in his neighborhood. And he was not alone: until the 1870s, there were few sources for food around St. Mary Magdalen's.

An 1879 advertisement.

By the 1870s however, the Italian colony in the southern part of Philadelphia was progressively taking on an appearance unlike other ethnic neighborhoods in the city. There was never a true ethnic homogeneity despite that the name, "Little Italy" was appropriate for the major ethnic group's representation. There were Eastern European Jewish immigrants, African Americans and native-born and some immigrants of British and German ancestries as neighbors. The newcomers assumed the rowhouse residences that previously belonged to the Irish, Catholic or Protestant. The Irish domination of this area spurred the construction of these rowhouses, the first House of Industry in Pennsylvania and an individual's identification with one's "corner" on which to loiter with one's peers.

St. Mary Magdalen de Pazzi Church, the first Italian national parish in the U.S., founded in 1852.

(photo by Michael Malloy)

The press noticed the increased migration to the area around St. Mary Magdalen's and recalled the former Moyamensing Township's reputation for slums, disease, blue-collar workers (if they did indeed work) and crime when the Irish were there.[8] With the influx of the Italian-speakers to the neighborhood, the economic class of the immigrants overshadowed any reference to Italian cooking as the "Mother of Western European Cuisine." Numerous macaroni dishes appeared in immigrant laborers bowls along with the ubiquitous Italian bread that had a variety of shapes and uses.

By the late 1870s and early 1880s, those who spoke Italian could now claim a nationality: Italian. And immigration to Philadelphia was encouraged with the promises for work and wealth. Likewise, more Italians came with the intention to settle and to join St. Mary Magdalen's: Neapolitans, Abruzzesi, Baresi, some Tuscans and a few from other regions were seen and heard around the church. "The Great Migration" brought macaroni dishes that varied by the immigrant's place of origin and availability of ingredients and finances. Some very simple recipes reflect the meagre lifestyle once experienced when a poor immigrant came to Philadelphia. All of these Italian regions are rich in traditional cuisine but some dishes are common to most areas in Italy.

Note: These are very common recipes and may be easily interpreted to individual tastes and imaginations.

MACARONI & LENTIL SOUP

6 C	water		1	onion, chopped
1¹/₂ C	dried & rinsed lentils		1	carrot, diced
1 C	celery, diced		1	garlic clove, diced
¹/₄ C	oil		1 t	salt & pepper (or to taste)
opt. tomatoes				

Sauté garlic and onion until slightly brown. Add water, lentils, onion, carrot, celery and optional tomatoes. Simmer on medium to low heat for about one hour.

Select a soup macaroni, like orzo or acini pepe and cook according to directions. Add to soup mixture after draining and stir.

Serves about four.

MACARONI & BEANS

5-6 C	water		2 T	oil
1 C	(or more) cooked small macaroni		2 C	(drained) white kidney or navy bean
¹/₂ t	minced garlic		¹/₂ C	onion, chopped
salt & pepper to taste			2 T	parsley
opt. basil			ham bone with trim	

Sauté garlic and onion until slightly brown. Add water, ham bone, salt, pepper and parsley and boil until stock is made. Add beans. Skim off any fat from top of soup. Remove about one-half of the cooked beans and pureé; return to stock. Add cooked macaroni and continue to simmer. Do not boil.

EGG SOUP

1 quart of fresh chicken stock	2	eggs
3 T chopped parsley	Parmesan cheese to taste	
salt & pepper to taste		

Simmer chicken stock while seasoning. Then bring to boil. In bowl, beat eggs with some cheese. Pour this into boiling stock, stirring consistently until egg is cooked within stock. Egg will appear first as cloudy. Bring stock down to cool. Sprinkle with cheese before serving.

Serves four to six, depending on appetite.

SPAGHETTI & ANCHOVIES

1 lb.	spaghetti	1 lb.	fresh anchovies without bones
2 T	oil	3 T	parsley
4	cloves of garlic, diced	salt & pepper to taste	

Prepare spaghetti according to package and drain. In skillet, sauté garlic in oil. Add parsley and stir until garlic starts to turn brown. Chop anchovies into small pieces and add to garlic and parsley mixture. Stir all into spaghetti. Sprinkle with some grated pecorino cheese.

Serves four.

SPAGHETTI AGLI'OL'
(with garlic & oil)

1 lb.	spaghetti or linguini	1/2	bulb (or more!) garlic diced small
1/4 C	olive oil	3 T	parsley
salt & pepper to taste		1 T	basil
opt. dried hot red peppers			

Cook macaroni according to directions and drain. Sauté garlic with oil, then add parsley, basil and other ingredients. Add mixture to macaroni and toss. For added spiciness, sprinkle dried hot red peppers atop and mix.

MACARONI & ONIONS

1 lb.	short or long macaroni	1/2 C	olive oil
3-4	onions, diced	salt & pepper to taste	

Sauté onions in oil until golden brown. On another burner, cook macaroni as directed and drain. Set aside. Add onions and oil and stir together. Sprinkle with any grated cheese.

Serves 4 to 6.

POLENTA

1 1/2 qts.	water	2 t	salt
1 1/2 C	polenta, ground		

Boil water and salt and gradually add polenta slowly, stirring to maintain consistency. Keep temperature to boiling until polenta is smooth in texture, then reduce heat . When cooled, polenta will be thick.

Serve polenta with any sauce that would be placed on macaroni. Cooled polenta can be fried, or baked. If not eaten immediately after cooling, refrigeration is recommended.

Serves about six.

PASTA RICOTTA

1 lb. cut macaroni cooked and drained $1^1/_2$ to 2 lbs. ricotta

grated parmesan or romano cheese   salt to taste

Cook macaroni according to directions and drain, leaving about 2 tbs. water in pot. Add ricotta and salt to taste and mix to consistency. Added cheese is optional. Serve while hot.

Serves four.

CHAPTER

The Neighborhoods,
Then the Markets
in Philadelphia's Italian Community

SOME OF THE RETICENCE OBSERVED in the early Italian groups who settled in South Philadelphia was eased as more immigrants began to dominate the neighborhood. Here, a confidence among the locals arose after nearly fifty years of an "ethnic occupation" that changed the brick facades of the rowhouses, church congregations and diets. St. Paul's Roman Catholic Church, founded in 1843 on the 900 block of Christian Street had been abandoned by Italian-speaking residents within the parish's boundaries not just because of linguistic and cultural differences but economic as well. St. Paul's, "The Irish Church," had a parish base of those with a more progressive lifestyle, compared to the immigrants. The Irish Catholics enjoyed some power within the Catholic diocese's hierarchy in Philadelphia, unlike the Italians. The Irish spoke English. The Irish acculturated faster. They were then, "Americans," more than any child born here of Italian parents. Joining St. Paul's was an accomplishment indeed to anyone from Italy or Sicily.

Sometimes though, there were problems within the neighborhood that emanated from the parish. Some of the foreign-born who ventured to go to St. Paul's encountered verbal as well as physical assaults.[9] But the same kind of courage that enabled the immigrant to cross the Atlantic Ocean caused him or her to surmount any fear of the "Americans" in the neighborhood. By 1900, and with a more secure standing, those of Italian and Sicilian ancestry became the majority at St. Paul's as more *'mericani* died or left the area.

As the "Americans" began to move southward and westward to newer neighborhoods, Italy sent more of its citizens to St. Paul's and Our Lady of Good Counsel's churches. Italian-speaking priests and nuns operated from the latter parish, just one block from St.Paul's, maintaining the linguistic tradition at church, school and in interactions outside of the ecclesiastical scope. Our Lady of Good Counsel Church, though, was the only site in the neighborhood that witnessed the nineteenth century immigrant's priorities.

The churches and employment were the forces behind the development of South Philadelphia's Italian colony and it is difficult to ignore these aspects of the local culture in relation to food. Residents in the neighborhood had been accustomed to shopping for food mostly outside of the area. Of the numerous markets in Philadelphia, there were none situated in the Italian colony until the 1880s. Called a "'Farmers and Butchers' Market," temporarily, this outdoor shopping area appeared on the north side of the intersection of Eighth and Christian Streets, near Cuneo & Lagomarsino's "Maccaroni Factory."[10] Produce was however sold at the Bainbridge or South Eleventh Street Markets, if not by wandering hucksters with their pushcarts. Eastern European Jews, intermingled with Italians and Sicilians, had their kosher foods at the South Fourth Street Market mostly. But eventually, Jewish grocery stores and butchers became located next to the Italian stores on the numbered streets and on Christian Street.[11]

The marketplace for food finally came to the neighborhood.

◆

Markets are interesting institutions and have been a part of Philadelphia since the city's founding in 1681. Back in the late 17th century, city planners designed varieties of markets to be established as the city's boundaries expanded. Markets such as the shed, open or curb appeared all over the city.[12] In 1888, there were forty-three markethouses in the city, all in relation to the urban setting.[13] Eight of these markets were located south of South Street and east of Broad. "The Farmers and Butchers Market," closest to the immigrant colonies at Eighth and Christian, was comprised of a concentration of stores that served those of mostly Italian ancestry and those not, notably the Jews from eastern Europe and Russia. Catharine, Carpenter, Montrose, Sixth and Seventh Streets likewise had a considerable number of food stores but what was evident then was that before 1890, there is variety

16

in foods; more occupations related to "fruits" and "produce" were commonplace to all ethnic groups.[14] And there was movement within the community which saw the former native-borns leave their homes for immigrants to occupy.

The Eastern European and Russian Jews by far added impact to the neighborhood with their foods. The kosher butcher, using his nickless blade in one sweep to slaughter, provided a service that was respected by the Gentiles who reciprocated by lighting candles or gas on the Sabbath. Ordinarily the Jew-Gentile relationships went well in "Little Italy" where Hebrew foods were sold next to the Italian products and would continue in one market venue after another in the neighborhood.

The Jews who settled more closely in the Southwark section, just northeast from St. Mary Magdalen's parish, managed to found a commercial strip around the South Fourth Street and South Street area which was more ethnically-homogeneous. Curbside stands, hucksters with carts and stores carrying kosher products eventually characterized South Fourth Street below Bainbridge as the market for the Jews of the Great Migration in this particular section of the city. Some advantages to this market were the pushcart vendors lining South Street from Delaware Avenue and the shed market that extended from Third to Fifth Street on Bainbridge Street. Success for these Jews guaranteed their independence from others.

Betty Zigerman Zolfstein, delivered by a midwife in 1908 survives as a testimony to recall a time when kosher stores in the neighborhood provided locals with the essentials for their cuisine. Betty's recipes reflect her Ukrainian Jewish ancestry with their ambiguous, yet creative tastes. She gives us the "staples":

BETTY'S CABBAGE SOUP

1	head cabbage, sliced and grated	1 t	sugar (more or less to taste)
1	(16 oz.) can whole tomatoes	1 t	"sour salt," (more or less to taste)
4 oz.	top rib	1	clove garlic (diced)
1 t	oil		

In a large, deep pot, sauté garlic and add top rib, "it gives it a little body," said Betty. Fill pot to about half with water and add cabbage, tomatoes, sugar and salt. Cook on medium heat until cabbage is limp. Serves 2 to 4.

BETTY'S BORSCHT

4 or 5	"nice size" beets	1	can tomatoes
1	medium onion	1 t	oil
1/2 C	lima beans	1	clove garlic, diced
1 C	potatoes, diced into small cubes	1 lb.	top rib (again, "for body")

"Sauté garlic in oil in large, deep pot. Add the top rib and brown on sides. Add water to fill half pot and boil top rib. Add diced beets, beans, onions and potatoes and place on medium heat until all are completely cooked. Add tomatoes last, then simmer."

Serves 2 to 4.

BETTY'S BRISKET

"It's not cheap, but it's good," said Betty. Be sure to go to a kosher butcher for the best cut.

One beef brisket	1 T oil
1 clove garlic, diced (plus 1/2 C more on side)	

Betty's directions:

"Trim fat off. Sauté garlic in oil and brown brisket on both sides in hot, large pot. Cut holes into the brisket and insert with garlic pieces. Put brisket in oven to bake on a slow flame for a few hours. Then, add potatoes and onions (the amount varies to one's preference) about one hour before brisket will be finished."

By the mid-1880s, there was an increase in the number of immigrants from Avellino and Campania who joined St. Mary Magdalen de Pazzi parish. C.C.A. Baldi, from the environs of Salerno, was by then an established name in Philadelphia's coal business after his stint in selling lemons. Baldi quickly became a community leader who assisted others from his hometown to migrate to Philadelphia. There was, however, a more prominent name in immigrant assistance from Campania, C. Antonio Marano (1853?- 1937) who brought a significant number of men and women from the mountain town of Montella, to the United States.

Mr. Marano was born in that little town in the clouds which carried the devotion of San Salvatore to South Philadelphia and to the suburban industrial town, Norristown in Montgomery County. Look inside of St. Mary Magdalen's or St. Paul's in Philadelphia or in Holy Saviour Church in Norristown and Mr. Marano's legacy is there: San Salvatore (Holy Saviour) who appeared in Montella. The "saint" bestowed extraordinary good graces on His devotees, as seen with Antonio Marano since his arrival in 1873. An enterprising man, Marano at first began to import Italian foods. He also provided local tanners with dog feces that were collected by the "doggie diamond pickers," hence, his nickname, "U Pellato," ("The Skin Man") from fellow Montellesi. Rohm and Haas developed a less expensive chemical for tanning and thus forced Marano to devote more time and energy towards importing a wider range of ethnic foods. "The Maranos, as importers, were all over," said Antonio's grandson, Luke Marano, Sr. Moreover, he said that his grandfather took a chance on expanding and came to ship Italian products to Italian communities "up and down the East Coast." But along with his travels to Italy for food, Antonio would bring fellow Montellesi to the U.S. on return trips. He then set the immigrants up in Philadelphia and in Norristown, where the jobs were. Eventually, he established a travel agency to organize the immigrations and then a bank in 1885, the "Banca Cooperativa" for the immigrants' savings.

Antonio Marano's contribution to the food industry in Philadelphia was more remarkable. Not only was he importing garlic from Mexico and Italy, but he increased domestic trade between California and Pennsylvania with olive oil and wine sales. Cotton oil was his best selling oil, as was Bertolli the imported Italian favorite. Business opportunities met Antonio Marano in strange ways, however. When he could not import macaroni during World War I, he bought John Wanamaker's former piano factory at Eleventh and Catharine Streets and started his own macaroni manufacturing, "The Philadelphia Macaroni Company." By then, no macaroni firm among the many around the neighborhood dominated local consumption. Cuneo and Lagomarsino's huge factory at Eighth and Christian Streets

C. Antonio Marano (1853-1937) one of Philadelphia "Little Italy's" most prominent food importers and manufacturers.
(Photo courtesy of Luke Marano, Sr.)

and Guano and Raggio's at Seventh and Montrose Streets held their own. By 1915, the Marano name attracted more consumers in proximity to the factory as well as businesses outside of Philadelphia which enhanced the owner's reputation for quality. Consequently, The Philadelphia Macaroni Company, under Antonio Marano was the first to manufacture the alphabet-shaped pasta for Campbell Soup, and would be in the Franco-American Spaghetti-Os, Lipton Soups and Knorr products. With this background of successes, it was no wonder that The Philadelphia Macaroni Company would be the first in the United States to make the college dormitory favorite, the ramen noodle, a "gelatinized" macaroni.[15]

Calling Antonio Marano's store a "Grocery" though, limits its impact on the neighborhood because this massive building at Seventh and Fitzwater Streets sold the essentials for Neapolitan cuisine as well as a better quality of Italian products that gave those from the region of Campania a chance to recreate the same dishes as in their homeland.

South-central Italian regional cooking was able to mature in South Philadelphia because there was a large population from both the Campania region's inland mountainous and coastal areas. The diversity in locations is evident in these settlers' cooking. Marano's store, plus an increased immigrant base at this time, guaranteed a supply of ingredients that would enliven anyone's palate.

19

Neapolitan cuisine in the Italian Market and its neighborhood has its foreign roots mostly in the cities of Naples and Salerno and the small town of Montella, about an hour's drive away. My aunt, Rose Morello Carfagno learned to cook from her mother-in-law, Rafaella, one of Antonio Marano's "imported" immigrants who became the main cook at "The Friendship Grill" in Bridgeport. This Neapolitan cooking tradition uses lots of a tomato sauce with the consistency and flow of a gravy. It coated everything: macaroni, meats, fish and vegetables. Aunt Rosie also used the same sauce atop her pizzas. Neapolitans tend to want to make their tomato sauce/gravy in "little time," as Salvatore Auriemma, owner of "Claudio's King of Cheese" said. "Thirty minutes—the whole thing— straight from the tomato!" No purées, no mixed purées with tomatoes.

Mozzarella and ricotta were other typical items incorporated into Neapolitan cooking, besides eaten alone. Salvatore noted a sheep's milk ricotta used extensively in his visit to Montella. Aunt Rosie, owner of M. Granese Fine Italian Cheese Company in Norristown will not contest her judicious use of her company's cheeses in so many of her Neapolitan dishes. She inherited recipes such as the famous Neapolitan Easter Pie, ricotta cake, lasagna, stuffed shells and others which the reader will have the opportunity to make, courtesy of the Italian Market neighbors. But first, Marie DiPopolo Miglino and her husband, Nick, the owners of "Felicia's" restaurant and both of Neapolitan ancestry have given these recipes which are appropriate to our case in point about this special cuisine.

THE MIGLINOS' GNOCCHI NAPOLITANI

1 lb.	whole milk ricotta cheese	1 egg	
1/2 t	salt	1 1/2 C flour	

"In a large bowl, mix the egg and salt until blended and then whisk in the ricotta until smooth. Place a scoop of ricotta mixture, the size of your fist, on a lightly-floured area. Sprinkle with flour and begin to roll until the ricotta forms a 'snake' the diameter of your finger. Cut the 'snake' into one inch pieces. Place on a floured cookie sheet. Refrigerate.

"To cook, bring 3 quarts of salted water to a boil. Cook the gnocchi for 2 to 3 minutes or until it rises to the top. Serves 4 to 6."

MIGLINO MARINARA NAPOLITANA

12 to 14 ripe plum tomatoes	2	cloves of garlic
3 or 4 leaves of fresh basil	6 T	olive oil
2 oz. fresh grated parmesan	salt and pepper to taste	

"Blanch the skins and seed the tomatoes. Heat the olive oil and add two minced garlic cloves and cook until a golden color. Add the tomatoes and cover with a lid for approximately 15 to 20 minutes. Season with salt and pepper. Chop the basil and add to the sauce. Let the sauce sit for 10 minutes, then combine it with the gnocchi in a bowl. Add the cheese and serve."

An anonymous fan of "The Saloon" restaurant submits this classic Neapolitan dish:

PENNE SESSO

1 lb.	Italian pork sausage, removed from casing (try Fiorella's)
3	hot peppers (long hots) diced in minute pieces
1	medium onion, diced finely 32 oz. prepared marinara sauce
4 oz.	flour 1 lb. cooked penne pasta

"Bring the sauce to a boil and add the remaining ingredients. Simmer for about one-half hour until the sausage is well done. This sauce will boil down as the water in the marinara sauce will evaporate. Serve atop the prepared penne."

Serves four.

Joseph DiGironimo, CFE, FMP of the JNA Culinary Institute created this Neapolitan dessert, appropriate for after eating something spicy.

JOSEPH DiGIRONIMO'S PARTENOPEA CASSATA GELATA

1 C	fresh strawberries 1/4 C chocolate chips
1 pt.	chocolate ice cream whipping cream
2 pts.	vanilla ice cream

"Slightly soften the ice cream to about the consistency of thick whipped cream. If the ice cream begins to get too soft, place in the refrigerator or freezer, if needed. Thinly slice about 1/2 C of the strawberries. Then, line a deep dome-shaped bowl (approx. 2 quarts) to about 1/3 of the way up the side with the sliced strawberries. Spoon 1 pint of the vanilla ice cream into the bowl, careful not to disturb the strawberries. Slightly smooth the top a bit and ever-so-gently press the ice cream down as you smooth. Place a few more of the sliced strawberries on top of the ice cream.

"Spoon 1 pint of the chocolate ice cream into the bowl. Again, slightly smooth the top a bit and ever-so-gently press the ice cream down as you smooth this level with the chocolate chips. Spoon the remaining pint of vanilla ice cream into the bowl as the top.

"Cover the bowl and palce it into your freezer; let sit until the ice cream is firm all the way through—4 hours at least but overnight would be best. Prepare a plate that is larger than the bowl by cutting the remaining strawberries into 'fans.' Remove the bowl from the freezer and place in a warm water bath for a second or so. Be careful not to let the water rise over the top. As the ice cream begins to soften, invert the bowl onto the center of your service plate. If needed, place the plate back in the freezer for a while longer. Just before service, garnish this cassata with whipped cream and the strawberry 'fans.'"

Michael DiPilla's great-uncle, Vincenzo "Jim" Nigro, born in 1907 used to pick produce on farms in New Jersey and sell them on 9th Street. His family was from Colliano and still makes this recipe which his grand-nephew said, "This is so good, you can't imagine!" A treat in the Naples area!

LILIANA ESPOSITO DiPILLA'S "PASTA ALLA GRIGLIA"

This can be made in a cast iron or aluminum pan with a cover. Or better yet, make this in a grill with a lid to keep the moisture inside.

10 round tomatoes	1/2 lb. locatelli cheese, grated
1 lb. dry long ziti	1/2 C olive oil
10 leaves of fresh basil	1 C water
salt to taste	ground black pepper "we use a lot because we like it hot!"

"Everything's in the pan—cut the tomatoes in quarters and line the entire pan with them. Hand-break the ziti into threes- that's what we usually do. Sprinkle the grated cheese on the next layer and pour 1/4 C of the olive oil on top. Lay the basil down. Then put on another layer of tomatoes, ziti, etc. Depending on the pan's size, keep making layers. Make the juices of the tomatoes go into everything.

"Pour the water over the top. Then put on the lid and bake on the grill for about an hour covered. Keep on a low heat to bake until the pasta is *al dente.*"

❧❧❧

No better way than to end this section on Philadelphia's Neapolitans than on this classic tomato sauce (or "gravy") as provided by Mr. James Campenella whose ancestors hailed from Naples.

This sauce can be used on anything: pastas, meats, vegetables, pizza, fish, polenta, sandwiches, eggs...anything!

JIM CAMPENELLA'S NEAPOLITAN-STYLE SAUCE

1/3 C	olive oil	1 1/2 C onion, finely chopped	
1	clove garlic, crushed	1 can (6 oz.) tomato paste	
1 T	sugar	2 T parsley, chopped	
1 t	dried basil leaves	1 T salt	
1 t	dried oregano leaves	1/4 t black pepper	
1 can (2 lb., 3 oz.) Italian tomatoes, undrained			

"In hot oil, in a 5 quart Dutch oven, sauté onions and garlic for 5 minutes. Mix in the rest of the sauce's ingredients and 1 1/2 C water, mashing tomatoes with a fork. Bring this to boiling; reduce the heat. Simmer, covered, stirring occasionally, for one hour."

This recipe goes with Jim's Manicotti and Cheese Filling in Part 2, p. 85.

State Senator Vincent J. Fumo, whose family's ties to the Italian Market go back decades, represents one of the local powers in the Market's future. He must be of Neapolitan ancestry—he has submitted this *haute cuisine* recipe, a fitting dish from this gentleman!

PENNE a la VINCENT

1	box penne, cooked & drained	1 large can, fat-free condensed cream
1/2 C	mushrooms, sliced thin	1 T garlic, chopped
1/4 lb.	plum tomatoes, chopped	"handful" parmesan cheese
	olive oil	parsley
1/4 C	white wine	crushed red pepper
2-3 stalks of steamed asparagus (tips only!)		

"Place enough olive oil to cover a deep sauté pan. Add the garlic, tomatoes, wine and sauté until tomatoes are soft. Then add the asparagus tips and mushrooms. Sauté for about 5 minutes until all are soft. Add cream, cheese and continue to sauté. Last, add the cooked and strained *al dente* pasta to the pan and toss.

"Add 1 t of crushed pepper seeds, salt, pepper and parsley. Eat this with Italian bread!"

"Bon appetite from Senator Fumo!"

The Great Migration's effects on local tastes was marked by a seeming explosion of occupations that connected food with St. Mary Magdalen's parish in the 1880s. There were just a few Italian restaurants on Spafford Street, near Sixth and Bainbridge,[16] but nothing of note that would have initiated more contacts beyond the neighborhood. Despite a proud number of parishioners who had migrated earlier from Liguria and who had realized the American dream, the immigrants from southern Italy who now took to settle in the parish placed more emphasis on food, their food, which they wanted to eat in this country. By the late 1880s, there were at least sixteen grocers and thirteen produce vendors in the parish with intentions of not being the "birds of-passage."[17]

The Ligurians, by about 1890, were a minority at St. Mary Magdalen's and were surpassed in tastes and food preferences there as well. The oysterman from the Naples area now was an occupation within the immigrant colony when more seafood was brought into the area and residents could afford it. Not too many of Italian ancestry were butchers, according to the business directories, but meats could have been sold inside of the grocery stores which served more as mini-supermarkets for locals. Food though, by 1890, finally became an outstanding feature to the "Little Italy" community which hosted immigrants from at least half

Pushcart vending in the smaller streets in "Little Italy." c. 1910

(Urban Archives. Temple University.)

of Italy's provinces. There was no "Little Naples" or "Little Abruzzi" or little anything to delineate the Italian colony further: everyone lived indiscriminately together, sometimes in blocks where some of Irish or German ancestries resided along with African Americans, Jews and even a few Chinese. Sicilians, though overtly linguistically estranged from mainland Italians, found themselves as "Italians" to the "outsiders."

Nevertheless, there still were within the community some rather minor effects of Italian regionalism which would best be considered as more of a matter of emotional comfort. Immigration brokers and boardinghouses were the reasonable consequences of mass migration because the local Catholic parishes, St. Mary Magdalen's and St. Paul's did not provide any type of social welfare programs. The House of Industry was limited in its services as was the Moyamensing Soup Society. Therefore, the immigration brokers, often called *padroni,* found the newcomers rooms in the large rowhouses to rent with the salaries they earned from the jobs that the brokers found for them. Brokers also charged the immigrants fees for every type of service: locating employers, translating verbally, appearances on behalf of the immigrant, reading letters or other documents, opening bank accounts, writing and sometimes selling food and drink.

Antonio Marano was one of the known brokers from the Naples area at St. Mary Magdalen's but the Abruzzesi at St. Paul's had another Antonio with the surname of Palumbo. At the immigrant processing station at Delaware and Washington Avenues, by the river, the newcomers bore pieces of paper pinned to their clothes which read, "Palumbo's, Philadelphia." In time, Abruzzese-style cooking would be served within private residences of the many local boardinghouses, such as Antonio Palumbo's and later at his "Hotel Palumbo." Almost at the same time, the DiRocco family's boardinghouse-turned-hotel would serve *la cucina abruzzese* at the "Corona di Ferro." This establishment survives today as "Dante & Luigi's Ristorante" at Tenth and Catharine Streets.

With the Abruzzesi, those of Italian ancestry in the South Philadelphia community were on their way towards making their kitchens in Philadelphia as theirs was in Italy. The bridges still exist between those of Abruzzese ancestry here and their distant relatives abroad. The D'Alfonso family are as others who have travelled to Abruzzese towns where migrations now are uncommon. Whereas Italian Market residents could cite Bucchianico, Ortona, Repa Teatina, Semivicoli, Vacri and Pennadomo as their forebearers' birthplaces, some connections remain constant. James Trovarello, a Federal agent who researched his family's geneaology, went beyond his Italian Market neighborhood roots. His paternal grandparents had followed the immigration route after hearing about Philadelphia from one of Palumbo's agents in their hometown of Bucchianico, near Chieti. Cesare and Lucia Trovarello arrived here in 1913 and 1914 respectively with the pinned labels. They would stay in Palumbo's boardinghouse for almost two years while working towards independent living.

The Trovarellos had left their "ancient hill town [that is] about 13 or 14 miles inland from the Adriatic," said their grandson who had visited and ate in his ancestral roots a number of times. In Philadelphia, Lucia brought her Abruzzese cuisine to the family table while Cesare introduced his tradition of making wine, the wine grapes which he would buy from Nick Marella at Ninth and Federal Streets in the Market.

James Trovarello, like Arata and Auriemma also enjoyed the ultimate genealogical experience by eating the same foods in the same environment of their ancestors. He savored the sights and tastes of the food that nourished generations before him. The Abruzzese dishes, according to Trovarello, are "just unbelievable...lots of grilled meats and grilled vegetables and lots of fresh fish." Tomato sauce is not too heavy in consistency and olive oil is a must in the diet. One of Trovarello's memorable dishes was this:

ABRUZZESE-STYLE SEAFOOD SALAD

2	dozen medium shrimp, shelled,deveined and cubed
1 lb.	fresh cod fillets
1/2 C	picante pepper, finely diced
	olive oil

Preheat oven to 350°F. In a pyrex baking dish, broil cod until it begins to separate. Remove from oven. While still warm, add the shrimp and pepper and drizzle with olive oil. Toss lightly and serve with fresh Italian bread—that is how Jim ate it!

Jim's Abruzzese cousin, Fernanda Santone was asked to give two family recipes which her American cousin has translated.

FERNANDA'S MINESTRA Di LENTICCHIE ABRUZZESE

1 lb.	lentils, dried and washed	1	stalk celery, chopped
2	cloves garlic, minced	3 qts.	chicken broth
7-8	plum tomatoes, cut in halves	4 T	olive oil
salt to taste			

"In a large pot, boil the broth. Add the celery, garlic and squeeze the juices from the tomatoes into the broth, then add in the tomato halves. Add oil and salt to taste. Add the lentils and reduce the heat. Cook for about 1 1/2 hours until the lentils are tender. If the soup appears too dry, add water. Sprinkle with grated cheese."

FERNANDA'S RISOTTO a la MARINARA ABRUZZESE

1 lb. arborio rice	8 oz.	calamari, cut into rings
8 oz. shrimp, deveined and peeled	8 oz.	crayfish or prawns
1 C white wine	32 oz. clam juice	
3/4 oz. sweet pepper, diced	1 clove garlic, minced	
pinch of crushed pepper	1 bunch parsley	
1 oz. butter (or 1/8 C)	salt to taste	
2 stalks celery, diced		

"In a frying pan, add 3 to 4 T olive oil and sauté the garlic, parsley and pepper together. Reduce the heat. Add all of the seafood and cook for 10 minutes. In a large pot, cook the rice with the wine until the wine is absorbed. Remove the seafood and add the juices from the pan to the pot with the rice. Over medium heat, add the clam juice, one cup at a time, stirring constantly, until it evaporates. This should take about 20 minutes. If the rice is still not tender, add boiling water. Turn off the heat, add the butter and stir.

"Pour the rice onto a platter and spoon the seafood on the top of the rice. Garnish with the parsley."

Fernanda substitutes conch (*scungilli*) and mussels, if the other types of seafood are not available.

Our current councilman, Frank DiCicco was born, raised and still lives and supports the 9th St. Market. His family was from Chieti in Abruzzi and contributed this recipe:

THE DiCICCO'S "PIZZA SOUP"

8 eggs, separated in two separate bowls

pinch of salt & pepper

"handful of parsley", chopped

1/2 C locatelli, grated

cooked chicken, in pieces

parsley for garnish

"handful of flour"

3-4   slices prosciutto, diced

2 qts. chicken broth

2 carrots, diced

In the bowl with the beaten yolks, combine the parsley, locatelli, flour and prosciutto. Beat the egg whites until peaks form, then fold in the yolk mixture. Blend to consistency.

"Put all in a round baking pan that has been sprayed with a non-stick coating. Bake at 350°F until the top is lightly brown. Insert a toothpick to check if it is still moist inside." Cook longer, if necessary. Baking time might be 25 minutes. Cool and set aside.

"Cut through the center of this bread-like mix into four (4) sections and then dice into little squares about 1" wide."

"Heat up the chicken broth, throw in the chicken parts, carrots and parsley and cook until carrots are done. Then, throw in the pizza parts and serve."

Makes about four servings.

Richard Gilberti, a life-long resident of the Italian Market, Executive Director of the Italian Market Civic Association for ten years and avid cook of his Abruzzese heritage has lent one of his family's favorites.

RICHARD GILBERTI'S RICE WITH MEATBALLS

1 C   long grain white rice or better, arborio rice

2 T   red tomato sauce

1/2 lb. ground veal

salt and pepper

1/2 C parmesan cheese

3 slices American bread or the "insides" or 3 slices of Italian bread soaked in milk

5 C   chicken broth

2 eggs, beaten

1 egg

onion powder to taste

blended oil to fry

"Make the meatballs by combining the veal with the bread, cheese, onion powder, salt, pepper and egg. Make meatballs about 1/2" in diameter. Fry lightly, then let meatballs drain on a paper towel.

"Boil rice as directed in chicken stock until done and set aside. Add the tomato sauce and stir. Beat the two eggs into the rice and add the meatballs, still stirring. Serve while hot."

Serves at least four as an entrée.

Mrs. Domenic Fante began life as Emilia D'Orazio, no relation to the D'Orazio Cheese family. She is still with us, having been born in 1902. Her family was from Abruzzi, too and brought this recipe.

EMILIA FANTE'S ROASTED CHICKEN WITH POTATOES

3-4 lb. roaster	2 garlic cloves
Italian parsley to taste	rosemary to taste
shortening	salt & pepper to taste
olive oil	
4-5 medium white potatoes, cut in quarters	

"Part-boil the potatoes for several minutes. Drain from water. Prepare chicken for roasting by first rinsing the chicken in salt water. Dry chicken. Sprinkle salt and pepper in the cavity, then insert 2 T shortening, the garlic, parsley and rosemary. Close with a skewer. Tie the wings together and cut off the tips of the wings.

"Grease the outside of the chicken with the shortening and sprinkle with more salt and pepper to taste. Tie the legs together. Lastly, drizzle the chicken with some olive oil and bake in a preheated oven at 350°F for 2½ hours uncovered. After the chicken has been in the oven for one hour, add the potatoes, sprinkle with salt and pepper, if desired, and continue baking."

⁕⁕⁕⁕⁕

Bread, as the substance of living, was always found in the homes of immigrants as well as the native-born. But what is not known is who of the Italians in Philadelphia's "Little Italy" community was baking bread first as a business. In the 1880s, bread may have been sold by the ubiquitous grocers in the neighborhood. The documentation shows that some of Italian extraction took to baking as an occupation in the immigrant colony later than expected. Stephen Diorio and Joseph Sassa were listed among the few of Italian ancestry in Philadelphia at that time to plunge into a job which was usually held and was well-established by those with German connections.[18]

Most of the bakers in the city in the 19th century were German-influenced, whether they were Amish, Mennonite, from the Rhineland, trained by those from these areas or anywhere the German language was spoken. This fact correlates to the extent of the history of Philadelphia's first German-speaking settlers who arrived at the earliest, in the 17th century. Given that the Italian-speaking population was insignificant in number with the rest in Philadelphia, many laborers may have still hoped to be self-employed as a baker someday. Quick macaroni-making took priority over the bread-baking process that took hours in preparation and more equipment to buy and maintain.

Hence, the delay in Italian bread bakers.

Nicholas A, Marinelli's bakery at 8th and Kimball Streets proudly delivered bread throughout the neighborhod by about 1903. Today, this company is known as "Vilotti-Pisanelli." (Photo by Brocato)

An oral history though, has that in 1898, Nicola Marinelli opened his bakery in a small rowhouse at Eighth and Kimball Streets for some in the neighborhood with no time to bake. It was convenient for the day workers who had to leave early in the morning to be trucked off for roadwork locally or to New Jersey to work in the farms. Mothers with large families could rely on bakers to do what time would not allow, if they could afford it.

Every baker has his own "signature bread" which differs from others with a slight use of certain ingredients or with the procedure. Some bakers claim that the type of heat determines the bread's texture. Simple Italian bread requires no special attention, as this recipe suggests. Using whole wheat flour may pose some caution in the baking process. Fennel seed bread is a traditional favorite if adding the seeds to the dough is desired.

ITALIAN BREAD

(Makes one loaf)

5 to 5 1/2 C flour—an all-purpose or part whole wheat is also good

3	eggs (opt.)	1 t salt
2	packages of yeast	water on side (about 2 C)
1 t	sugar	1 stick unsalted butter or soft
1 1/4 C hot milk (not scalding or boiling)		margarine

Sprinkle yeast and sugar in ¼ C milk and let dissolve. Yeast will form a foam after a few minutes. In a bowl, place 1 C milk with butter and salt and stir to consistency. Then, add beaten eggs, foamy yeast and gradually add flour, one cup at a time until dough forms.

Throw some flour onto your kneading surface and place dough on surface for first kneading. Add necessary flour to surface to avoid any sticking. Dough should remain soft but not sticky.

After this first kneading, put dough in a greased bowl and cover to increase heat. Dough will be left to rise for about 1¼ hours or until it doubles in size.

Remove dough from bowl and knead again on floured surface. Repeat "warming and rising" as above for about 1 hour. Then place dough into a greased and floured bread pan. Preheat oven at 350° F. Brush top of bread with a beaten egg and water mix, if a "glazed" look is desired. Bake bread until edges turn brown. When finished baking, cool outside of oven.

❦

By 1900, St. Mary Magdalen's and St. Paul's parishes had some relief in the overwhelming immigrant population with the founding of Our Lady of Good Counsel Church in 1898. It was located on the south side of the 800 block of Christian Street by the Italian Provincial of the Augustinians. Italian-speaking priests introduced Italian-speaking nuns to a ministry within a congested urban environment that had by that time, lots of food bought, sold and cooked. There was the opposite side, across the street from the church and rectory where the hucksters hawked their wares. Busy Christian Street, named after the seventeenth century Swedish queen and unusually wide and well-trodden became the venue for food now: The "Farmers and Butchers Market" at Eighth and Christian had long faded into oblivion by the end of the century.

In 1897, Philadelphia had forty-one "Markethouses" with the closest one to the South Philadelphia Italians on South Eleventh Street.[19] The established markets were still standing and doing well with a prominent immigrant clientele, but now the newcomers who moved southward could also shop at "1632 Passyunk Avenue," six long blocks below Washington Avenue.[20] If they did shop there, they were the minority among native-borns who left homes in the older section, northeast, or "up the Passyunk." Moyamensing Prison, built in 1837, incarcerating men and women and carrying out executions, stood on Passyunk Avenue midway between market places, dividing neighborhoods and neighbors.

The number of Jews from Russia was competitive with the Italians and Sicilians in the same areas by 1900. But the mobility of the one group versus the others was in different directions. The Jews moved generally in a northern or southern orientation, hugging close to the Delaware River while the Italians and Sicilians moved westward and southwestward more at this time, encountering the "Syrians," just below Washington Avenue.

They were classified as "Syrians" but they were really Lebanese, the Maronite Catholics who arrived in South Philadelphia in the 1860s to flee from mass slaughter in the Middle East. Over one million Maronite Catholics were killed by Muslim Druze; those who found refuge in the mountains survived, then migrated to the United States. In 1861, the first Maronite Catholic Church in the U.S., St. Maron's, was founded in Philadelphia at Tenth and Ellsworth Streets. In 1898, the first Arabic newspaper in the U.S., *Al-Hoda,* was begun at 1014 Ellsworth.[21] Consequently, by 1900, almost one hundred "Syrians" were living next door to the immigrant Italians and Sicilians within St. Paul's parish during the Great Migration.[22]

Food for the Lebanese however, was in the offing for others to taste as well as to purchase. While many Lebanese claimed to be "salesmen"[23] of a sort, their cuisine was limited to their own within their community, not to the public. "Lebanese immigrants' food then was the same as today," said Mr. James Tayoun. Lamb, the main meat used in Middle Eastern cuisine was "cheap and went a long way," he added. Pieces of leftover lamb were used in shishkabob with vegetables easily bought by Italian produce hucksters. But there were the staples of Middle Eastern cuisine that remained guarded from non-Middle Easterners for decades, such as *khdz* or in Arabic, *aish,* which is known more vernacularly as "pita." Later, with more importation of foods to the area came the sesame seeds to make *tahini,* oils and spices that characterize Middle Eastern cuisine. Hummus is made of garbanzo beans, the ceci peas to Italians, one of the few culinary "bonds" to their neighbors from the central part of the Mediterranean.

Mr. James Tayoun, born and raised in this Lebanese-Italian community and owner of only the second Middle Eastern restaurant in Philadelphia provided these recipes which are typical of traditional Lebanese cuisine:

BABA GHANNUJ
(Eggplant Appetizer)

1	large eggplant, peeled and cut into 1" cubes
1	clove garlic, smashed
1/2 t	salt to taste
4 T	*tahini* (can be purchased at any Middle Eastern grocery)
1/2 C	water
1/4 C	lemon juice, or more if desired
1/4 C	finely chopped parsley and pomegranate seeds
1 T	olive oil and *simmaq,* both optional or to taste

Over medium temperature, cook eggplant in a pan with some water until done. Set aside. In wooden bowl, blend garlic, salt and tahini together, adding some water, if necessary, for consistency. Last, add lemon juice and mix. Then add eggplant to bowl and with a masher (or Arab *mdaqqa*) or pestle, mash and blend the ingredients. Traditional Middle Eastern cooks use parsley or pomegranate seeds as a decorative "trim." Arabs also tend to drizzle a good olive oil atop the appetizer. Or use *simmaq*.

This recipe was intended to be a dip, which would use a food processor or blender to mix the ingredients for a smoother texture.

MNAZLIT BATINJAN
(Eggplant & Chickpea Stew)

1 large eggplant, peeled and cut into small cubes

1/2 C	chopped onion	1	clove garlic
1/2 C	olive oil	1-2 C	water (or more)
1	(16 oz.) can chickpeas	2 T	parsley, chopped
1	can (16 oz.) whole tomatoes	1/8 t	cumin

salt and pepper to taste

On medium heat, sauté onions in oil in deep pan. Add remaining ingredients and continue to cook for 15 to 20 minutes, occasionally stirring. Do not boil. Serves about 4 adults either hot or cold, atop rice or alone.

LUBYI biz-ZAYT
(Green Beans)

1 (oz.) can tomato sauce		1 lb.	fresh or canned beans
1 clove garlic, chopped		1 medium onion (1/3 C) diced	
2 T	oil	1/2 C	water
salt			

Cook beans until tender. Sauté garlic and onion in oil in frying pan until soft but not browned. Add cooked beans and tomato sauce and continue to cook over medium heat, adding water only if necessary. Serve when mixture is thoroughly heated but not boiling. Serves about four as a side dish.

LEBANESE EGG OMELET

4-5	eggs, beaten	1/2 C	milk
1/2 C	chopped onion	1/2 C	parsley, chopped
1/2 C	chopped scallions	1/4 t	mint, if desired
3-4 T	oil	salt and pepper to taste	

Set oven at 350°F. Coat a cooking dish with oil and place in oven to get hot. In bowl, beat eggs and milk then add dry ingredients and mix well. Pour into the hot baking dish from the oven and return to oven to bake eggs until edges turn brown. Cut and serve as main or side dish.

FAVA BEAN PATTIES

1 T	flour	1/2 C	cooking oil
1/4-1/2 C	onion	2 cloves garlic, diced
1 t	ground coriander	1/2 t	cumin
1/4 t	hot pepper	1 t	baking soda
salt and pepper to taste	1 lb.	fava beans

Place whole fava beans in cold water for 3 to 4 days before cooking this dish, draining and replacing water each eay. In a food processor, mix peeled favas, onions and remaining ingredients until smooth. Make patties of mix and place in frying pan with oil. Serve in bread as a sandwich or meatball-style.

It's the year, 1900 and the place to shop for food in "Little Italy" is on the north side of the 800 block of Christian Street. Pushcarts begin to line about the curbs in front of stores or residences. Our Lady of Good Counsel's tremendous growth as a parish outnumbered St. Paul's and St. Mary Magdalen's, guaranteeing customers for Christian Street merchants: parishioners could stop and buy after church services. It was a convenience.

Christian Street's other advantages though were conducive for good business: it linked neighborhood traffic; it was very wide, unlike the other streets; and it was not far from the main food-transporting roadways. Christian Street runs in an east-west direction, from the Delaware River to the Schuylkill River. From its earliest construction, this street was intended to be a thoroughfare for then-Southwark, Moyamensing and Passyunk Townships because "Prime" or Washington Avenue to the south, carried on more industry with the factories, foundries, coal yards and other businesses which were not compatible with residential developments. Southwark's and Moyamensing's township buildings were on Christian Street as were some churches and other buildings of community interest.

By the time that an "Italian section" of the city was recognized however, Christian Street's potential was realized especially with the number of large rowhouses that often sheltered innumerable residents and a church where scores of baptisms per month steadily increased the neighborhood's growth.[24] It was not unusual to find more than twenty (20) individuals per rowhouse.[25] Nor, at this time was it uncommon for some class division within the community. A first-generation U.S.-born class of children born to immigrant parents represented their parents' intention to stay and to do well. But this group stood in contrast to recent immigrants who yet had to try to acculturate. While St. Paul's and St. Mary Magdalen's now had among their parish base those who desired to stay and those

Shopping along 800 block of Christian Street, c. 1904, "THE 'Italian Market'" until 1930.

(Urban Archives. Temple University.)

with comfortable lifestyles and occupations, Our Lady of Good Counsel's parishioners were mostly the very poor newcomers.

Here was Good Counsel nestled between St. Paul's and St. Mary Magdalen's and catering to the flux of immigrants who were almost twenty years behind the others of their ethnic group. Of these immigrants, most arrived from Calabria, Bari and eastern Sicily with smaller numbers still calling Abruzzi and Campania their home regions. Very few of the Calabresi, Baresi and eastern Siciliani were literate. All, to some degree were impoverished and barely made travel expenses. The majority left residences that generally were spared any element of civility. Some left "homes" that were hewn from the sides of hills; others renounced shacks made of scrap building material. Hardly anyone departed from these areas for a reason other than to work and to make money.

And once in the U.S., there was no desire to return.

For those who came during this migration period to Philadelphia, they knew that one trip across the Atlantic was all one needed. Immigrants already heard the stories that the streets were not paved with gold, that they may work under deplorable conditions for substandard wages and that they may be subject to a variety of abuses. Our Lady of Good Counsel was perhaps a place to go for assistance, at least with the Italian-speaking priests and *paesani* there.

An occupation around food was one way in which the illiterate and/or ignorant could survive, without having the necessary language skills. Many immigrants who were not employed by a large contracting company could walk down to Dock Street, buy some produce or fish and walk it back to the neighborhood to be sold. Children and the elderly did this to supplement family incomes but others saw this type of work as an independent means to work among their own on their own time and conditions. Food vendors often worked alongside of vendors with gadgets for the house, services such as sharpening knives and tools, repairing umbrellas and selling clothes and linens. The junk men and ragmen wanted the wood for pulp, the metals and even animal waste. Cries of "Bones!" or "Rags!" were heard competing with the choruses of "Fr-e-e-sh to-o-o-ma-a-toes!" and the coloraturas of the other vendors who made the names of some produce expand to several syllables, each with a different musical note.

If the vendor had some money, he bought a horse and wagon for more goods to sell. If he didn't have the means, he pushed his own wheeled cart, hence the name, "pushcart," a name seemingly coined by a neophyte to the English language.

CHAPTER

Local Shopping
&
The Great Migration

PUSHCARTS MOVED ERRANTLY around the neighborhood without any stationary intentions. Some pushcart vendors left their neighborhood to sell at other places while some men were content to stay localized. Along with Good Counsel's parish population were the other churches to create a population density that rivalled that of a small city. This is not to ignore those of other ethnic groups and the native-borns, many of whom lingered in the neighborhood despite its foreign cultural environment.

Fred Jacovini's son, the energetic Pietro (or Peter) was given the challenging position to perform some work for the U.S. Government in the neighborhood. Fred, who arrived from Calabria, had a grocery store on the 900 block of South Ninth Street when Peter began the task of taking the U.S. Census for his new country. It would be the first of many such honorary jobs that Peter would do in the city for his neighbors.

Peter Jacovini was an exemplary figure among not just the Calabresi but within the entire community. He later started a newspaper at 924 South Ninth Street called, "Il Popolo," still clutching onto the Italian language long after he was accepted by the native-born Philadelphia set. So well known was Peter Jacovini, that he was allowed to ride a white horse as the lead in the New Year's Day parade on Broad Street.

Such verve is typical of the regional cuisine that fed Peter Jacovini and other Calabrians. Centuries of Greek occupation, then an invasion by more Greeks and Turks in 1453 influenced the cooking of this area of Italy. Our Italian Market expert on Calabrian cooking is Frankie Perri, Jr., owner of "Frankie's At Night Eclipse" restaurant. "All of my menu is Calabrian. It is the only Italian food," he boasted. Three generations of Calabrians taught Frankie the essentials of this regional cuisine, although he credited his grandmother, Palmina Abruzzese Perri and Aunt Louise Sulpizio. Count his mother, Evelyn and father, Frank "Shanks" with their influences too—"Frank's 'Shanks' and Evelyn's" is known to every Center City lawyer who crave their "jumbot." It is also the preference of former neighborhood son, now U.S. Ambassador to Italy, our honored Honorable Thomas Foglietta.

Frankie explained Calabrian cooking as "more in depth with spice and with peppers, like Italian hot peppers. It's from the soul—the real Italian cooking." The Calabrian dishes provided in this section speak for themselves. Led by one of Frankie Perri's signature dishes, the boldness of Calabrian cuisine is expressed initially in the ingredients. The tastes are extraordinary!

FRANK PERRI, JR.'S CHICKEN & SHRIMP CALABRESE

1 lb.	chicken breasts, whole and split and pounded	3-4	"Colossal" shrimp, the "Beegees" — cleaned and deveined
1/4 C	blended oil or soy bean oil	4	cloves garlic, chopped
2 T	butter	10 oz.	real chicken stock
1 C	white wine (dry)	4 oz.	seafood stock
1 1/2 C	(or more) mushrooms, sliced 1/4" thick		
1 T	each "organically grown" fresh parsley, basil and oregano		
flour "to dust"		salt & pepper to taste	

"In a sauté pan, dust off the breasts with flour and sauté them in blended oil on both sides. Discard the oil. In the same pan, keep the meat and add the whole shrimp and 2 T butter. Add the salt, pepper and mushrooms, parsley, basil and oregano. Sauté until garlic is golden. Then hit it with the dry white wine. Cook it off til the wine disappears. Add the stock, then boil until the stock thickens and is reduced."

Frankie suggested to serve this with pasta aglio ed'olio and a salad. A pinot griglio wine was Frankie's first choice.

Marc A. Houad learned to cook Calabrese from his relatives who came from Reggio Calabria, the Laganas. Raised in the Italian Market neighborhood, Marc's other cultural heritage is Lebanese. He is a funeral assistant with the Jacovini and Baldi families.

Marc's home-made wine is yet unavailable for sale, but his Calabrian dish would go wonderfully he said, with either a Trebbiano or a pinot griglio.

MARC A. HOUAD'S SPAGHETTI WITH SWORDFISH CALABRESE

1 lb.	swordfish, cut into cubes	4-5	hot dried chili peppers
6 T	virgin olive oil	6	ripe plum tomatoes, chopped
2	cloves garlic, thinly sliced	1/2 C	dry white wine
2 T	capers	1 lb.	spaghetti, cooked
1/2 C	assorted basil, oregano and pinch of mint	2 T	chopped Italian *flat leaf* parsley
10-15	black pitted olives, oil cured, chopped		

"Season fish with the salt and fresh ground pepper. Boil water for the pasta. In a sauté pan, heat the oil, garlic and peppers. Throw in the fish and toss. Do not brown. Add the tomatoes and wine. Then add the seasoning with the olives and capers.

"Pour this atop the pasta and toss. Garnish with the flat leaf Italian parsley."

Connie Tirotti Borriello's family is everywhere in and around the Italian Market. Her son, Paul added that his family had "fruit and produce businesses all up and down 9th Street." Connie's family was from Cutro in Calabria—she makes this dish, "It's the easiest thing!" Her son the realtor recalls this as the meal that the bookies ate while playing the numbers at "The Pushcart Saloon."

CONNIE TIROTTI BORRIELLO'S PASTA CEC'

2 T	olive oil	1	medium onion, diced
16 oz.	can ceci peas (chickpeas)	1 lb.	elbow macaroni
3	cloves garlic, diced	2 T	basil
8 oz.	tomato paste	1 t	oregano
8 oz.	chopped tomatoes (from the can)		salt & pepper to taste

"It's all in one pan! Get a large saucepan and heat the olive oil and brown the garlic and onions. Then add the tomato paste and stir. Add 1 C tomatoes. Boil. Add one can of chickpeas (ceci) with water and cook for a short time over a medium flame. Add the uncooked elbow macaroni. Wait until the pasta explodes in the pan. Now serve it." Easy.

CHAPTER

The "Italian Market"
is born on
South Ninth Street

THE 9TH STREET ITALIAN MARKET did not exist in 1900 but there were some indications that vendors were interested in the potential of 9th Street. Judging from the census, the street appeared no more remarkable than the other numbered streets in the neighborhood which now counted more of Italian and Sicilian ancestries than any other nation of origin. There was a number of Jews, mainly from what boundaries comprised of a "Russia". These individuals, as well as the remaining native-born were also involved in the food businesses with their general stores or, butcher stores, but no other ethnic-based food emporium.

By 1900 though, there are more Italian immigrants joining St. Paul's, the "Irish Church" which had some of its American parishioners trying to block the newcomers' entry to one of the only interests for the immigrants. One oral history has that Salvatore Lucchesi from the tiny seacoast village of Spadafora, Sicily was the first to set up a stand on the corner of 9th and Christian Streets. A young man, Lucchesi sold fish and had influenced others from Spadafora to do the same near him. One of the obstacles to verifying this "history" however, is the absence of Lucchesi's name in any document to corroborate it. There are no records to prove where he was living at the time cited in the oral history and certainly no written proof on any street vendor.

What is true is that Lucchesi fought to join St. Paul's and his sons continued to fend off any armed parishioner who tried to stop the Lucchesis from attending church services or school. Whereas other Spadaforesi went to Our Lady of Good Counsel, the Lucchesi family persevered at St. Paul's.

My personal belief about these first pushcart vendors is that they took to "itinerant vending" because they were without the means to purchase or to rent a place for business. Moving about in the streets caused some traffic, maybe some competi-

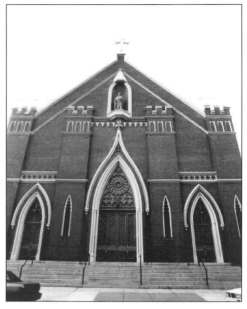

St. Paul's Church, founded in 1843, the church of the The 9th Street "Italian Market." (Photo by Mike Malloy)

tion for a choice space on some corners or high volume stores. The pushcart allowed the immigrant vendor the mobility to go to other streets where there might be no competition. With the low degree of liability, the poor immigrant pushing the cart of goods had very little to worry about because he could keep moving.

There is no evidence to suggest that 9th Street in 1900, or even in 1905 was of any note. At least by those years, some of those Italians from St. Mary Magdalen de Pazzi who acclimated to U.S. culture called 9th Street near-Christian, "Il Quartiero Italiano,"[26] an acknowledgement of some type to the ones who fled the direst of situations abroad. Only one individual among the newcomers on 9th Street was considered a cut above the rest of those from Spadafora: Pietro Giunta, Lucchesi's *paesano*.[27] With Giunta, the non-Sicilian community recognized a leader among a group of individuals that would have gone unnoticed in Sicily.

Spadafora lies on the northeast coast of Sicily in the province of Messina. The name, "back outside" is from the Latin. Most of the residents of this quaint village of two to three thousand probably originated from the city of Messina long ago. Facing the Tyrrhenian Sea, Spadafora's shores gave its people its main occupation, fishing. In the U.S. however, the Spadaforesi found that selling fish was not lucrative enough, so other food-related occupations were tried. After 1900, with many immigrants from Spadafora at Our Lady of Good Counsel and St. Paul's, produce vending, baking and butchering, along with the selling of fish thrived around 9th and Christian Streets.

There may be reasons why 9th Street's Market derived from the 800 block of Christian Street. From my analyses, Good Counsel attracted most of the immigrants from southern Italy and Sicily with St. Paul's running close in second place in its parishioner base. St. Mary Magdalen's numbers did not correlate to these churches' growing figures which some have attributed to interethnic conflicts. St. Paul's could not be restrictive in its admission of parishioners because as a "territorial parish" it had to accept any Catholic within its boundaries. On the contrary, Good Counsel and St. Mary's were "national parishes" and were founded upon a foreign language as a means of communicating God's Word. St. Paul's position with the Archdiocese by 1900 drew more specialized programs that would promote immigrant services and try to make the immigrants there feel more comfortable.[28] Certainly, by 1900, the majority of Irish Americans at St. Paul's had been in decline and mobilized in south and westward directions. With immigrants at St. Paul's doling out to the church, the Archdiocese was forced to recognize the new type of parishioner that would be maintaining this parish. The Trinitarian Sisters, Salesians and later the Franciscan Missionaries of the Sacred Heart and Norbertines swelled in numbers to service the Catholics of Italian and Sicilian ancestries at St. Paul's.[29] Their work force already showed future promise: the Archbishop Patrick Ryan School at St. Paul's was built in 1905 to accommodate 2,000 young students.[30]

This religious, yet welcoming presence at St. Paul's may have been the primary indication for the increase in population and food-related businesses in the neighborhood. By 1900, any product from Italy probably could be purchased here, or at the least, imported easily. There were the oils, spices, herbs, vegetables that were now grown in New Jersey or in suburban Philadelphia, the imported meats and baccalà. Italians sought to bring as much from abroad, including the fig tree and produce such as the *cucuzzi, finocchio* and *broccoli rabe.*

Giacomo Foti from Riposto, in southeastern Sicily, rose from street hawker to the proprietor of his own importing business in Philadelphia which he named after his wife, Rosa. It was 1903 and importing food from Italy was commonplace, unlike decades before when Antonio Marano broke into areas of food importing which no one had yet done. Giacomo Foti was regarded as with other Sicilians, as more "business-like" than the mainland Italians. It seemed as if more men from Sicily were engaging in self-employment rather than long-term labor for others. Paesani kept close usually to other paesani, even among the others in the same province or region. But generally Sicilians, with their own language that somewhat separated them from mainland Italians, kept to themselves. Some Sicilians began farms in New Jersey to raise produce to sell in the city. Other Sicilians saw a way to have a "business'" from their pushcart at a favorite site on 9th Street which was, seemingly, like a frontier land awaiting settlement. Records do show the names of store owners and residents on 9th Street, but census takers could not take the names of the many Sicilian pushcart vendors.

Giacomo Foti progressed past the pushcart, but there still were scores of these men wanting the next best to sole proprietorship.

A wheel on the pushcart was its movement to and from the docks on the Delaware River to the 9th Street Market. The wheel was proof that the pushcart owner was at a site temporarily. The vendor might move his "place of business" elsewhere at will, but preferred to be on a wide, well-traveled street, near others from his hometown or near others who ventured to do the same. Pushcarts moved along, with or without a song, always with a prospect ahead. If they chose to be stationary, pushcarts could rest in front of a busy store and perhaps benefit from the flow of customers.

The Sicilians who settled in the "Little Italy" neighborhood just before and after 1900 were largely from the eastern half of the island of Sicily. The Provinces of Messina and Catania claimed the most immigrants with the cities of San Pietro, Giardini, Calatabiano, Sant'Alfio, Francavilla, Messina, Catania and Syracuse all represented in the businesses at the Market.[31] The Province of Palermo sent only a minimal number to Philadelphia from Caccamo and the towns just outside the city of Palermo. The Greeks who settled in eastern Sicily developed a culinary tradition with the indigenous plants there as well as with the olive and grape, probably by the Fifth Century B.C. when Syracuse rivalled with Athens in almost every level of civilization. Sicily's Muslim ties that began more seriously in the 9th century brought sugar, dates, cinnamon, citrus and couscous from their North African culinary roots.

When eating in Sicily, one will notice native influences and find little support for the claim that Sicily's many invaders left their traces. Most of these "invaders"

Lucchesi's Seafood was on corner at far left; but Anastasi's on right will continue in the next century.

touched the island, but to be sure, settlement is another matter. The Greeks settled here, the Normans and French from Province settled here after the Muslims left indelible marks—these are evident in Sicilian cuisine.

Charles Cannuli, Sr. of "Cannuli's House of Pork" on 9th Street got to sample a delicately spiced roasted pig in eastern Sicily that was reminiscent of what he sells. His Sicilian-style pork was inspired by his mother, Antoinette's recipe which she learned from her Messinese parents. Mr. Cannuli found that the Sicilian cooking in the eastern part of the island was not dominated with tomato. I saw and ate similarly in the western part of the island. But there are the tell-tale signs of Sicilian cooking—it has often been said that Sicilians can make soup from a rock. But is it characteristically, "Sicilian"? Sicilians generally can make anything edible, more edible with a few simple ways. Except when it comes to pastries! (That's another story!)

Judge Sicilian cuisine by these recipes that have been handed down within the families of Italian Market merchants and neighbors. Let us begin with Rosemarie Anastasio LaRosa, a descendant of the Spadaforesi.

ROE LaROSA'S TUNIN' (FRESH TUNA)

4 slices fresh tuna, 1/2" thick	1 medium onion, diced
1/2 C balsamic vinegar	cooking oil for frying

"In a large skillet, heat the oil and sauté onions until they carmelize. Add 1 T vinegar. Remove the onions and put on the side. In the same skillet, sauté the tuna on both sides, but do not burn the fillets. Return the onions to the cooked tuna and put the remaining vinegar on top. Continue to cook for 10 minutes more.

Roe said, "It is a must! Tomatoes, fresh basil and red bermuda onions" bathed in balsamic vinegar, olive oil, salt and pepper as a side dish. She also recommends asparagus to accompany the fish.

Rosalie LaRosa Fornia's mother was from Belmonte Mezzagno, just outside of Palermo in western Sicily. This recipe came to Philadelphia in 1922 when Angelina, Rosalie's mother migrated. "My mother made it with such love," sighed Rosalie. This was a frequent dish on the LaRosa table.

ANGELINA LaROSA'S PASTA chi FINOCCHI e SARDE

1 lb. fresh sardines (or canned)	4 T olive oil
4 bulbs of fennel with attached greens	1/2 C golden raisins
1 large onion, chopped	4 cloves garlic, chopped
1/2 C capers	salt & pepper to taste
1/2 C Italian seasoned breadcrumbs	olive oil to fry

In a sauté pan, "brown the breadcrumbs fast in olive oil. Remove. In a saucepan, sauté onions and garlic until golden. Clean and chop the leaves on the fennel, but use only one bulb and chop it very, very fine. Add this with the oil, garlic and onions. Then add 1 C water, salt and pepper, raisins, capers and sardines. Let it simmer for one hour on a low heat. Check for water to add as it cooks. Let this cook so that the flavors have to marry each other." A sauce will develop.

"Pour one-half of this sauce on the pasta and mix. Then, pour the other half of the sauce on top. Sprinkle with the breadcrumbs. You can add cheese on top" if one desires.

Eastern Sicilian cooking traditions die hard at the Italian Market because so many good cooks were born of these Spadaforesi and others with roots in that part of the island. Chef Instructor Michael DeLuca used his birthright in cooking along with his imagination in this, one of his creations.

MICHAEL DeLUCA'S VEAL CATHERINE

8 oz.	veal medallions, cut into two (4 oz.) pieces		
16-20	shrimp	4 oz.	lump crabmeat
1	plum tomato, diced	1/4 C	white wine
1/4 C	chicken broth or stock	1 t	tabasco sauce
1 T	granulated garlic	1/4	(wedge) lemon, squeezed
1/8 lb.	butter		salt and pepper to taste
flour to dust			fresh parsley
oil to fry			

"Dredge the veal in flour and sear until lightly browned. Remove. Flash fry the shrimp until half done. Remove. Drain the oil. Put the pan back on the fire and add some butter. Sauté the plum tomatoes. Deglaze with wine. Add the shrimp and veal with the tabasco, garlic, salt and pepper. Simmer for two to three minutes. Add the stock and continue to simmer for two to three minutes more. Finish with crabmeat and butter."

"Serve and enjoy!" Makes two servings.

Holidaytime with Sicilians can be an extravagant lay-out of foods. The Cardullo family originated from Messina. It is the name of the family who sells fuel oil in the winter and water ice (or "Italian ices") as soon as the warm weather appears. Barbara and Carol Cardullo submitted these recipes that they make, Sicilian-style at home.

CARDULLO'S CHRISTMAS EVE FISH SALAD

1 lb.	shrimp, broiled	6	lobster tails, broiled
1	can jumbo lump crabmeat, cleaned	1	clove garlic, chopped
1 lb.	calamari rings, broiled	1/4 C	olive oil
juice of 3 lemons			fresh parsley to taste
salt and pepper			

"In a bowl, place the fish and add the garlic, lemon juices, oil, salt and pepper and parsley." Refrigerate.

The ladies suggest that this dish should be served chilled.

An encore from the Cardullo women:

CARDULLO'S EGGGLANTS OVER PASTA

The Marinara Sauce:

3-4	cloves garlic	2 T	olive oil
1 can	crushed tomatoes		fresh parsley to taste
1 T	basil		salt and pepper to taste

"Sauté the garlic in enough olive oil to coat the pan. Add one can of crushed tomatoes, the salt, pepper, fresh parsley and fresh basil to taste."

one large eggplant	salt
blended oil	locatelli cheese, grated
long pasta, like spaghetti or linguini	

"Slice the eggplant to about 1/4-1/2" thick. Salt the eggplant and let it drain on a paper towel."

In a skillet, "fast fry" the eggplant in the oil until they are brown.

In a baking pan, layer these eggplants with the marinara sauce and locatelli cheese. End with the cheese on top. Bake for 1/2 hour at 350°F then serve over the prepared macaroni.

Serves about 4.

It is difficult to pinpoint an exact year for the "birth" of the 9th Street Market. The street had been functioning, as most major streets, with businesses on the first floor and residences above. At least that was how the majority of the buildings were planned from the 700 block south to the 1200 block. But to call 9th Street a "market" would still be far from fact even in 1905. There were miscellaneous stores on 9th Street that were not food-related, such as Domenico Fante's furniture and the druggists, hardware and repair shops. In front of these stores, may be some pushcarts, moving about at various times. But no documentation survives, only oral histories which recall mobile and immobile carts going about on the streets.

The tendency for the pushcarts to gravitate towards 9th Street was probably coincidental. Some tales that the Sicilians were forced to go there and away from Christian Street have no substance of truth. Sicilians comprised a significant group of parishioners at Our Lady of Good Counsel Church, so they belonged, as some have said. Ninth Street was a reasonable, negotiable venue for parishioners of both St. Paul's and Good Counsel to ply their goods. Some businesspersons on 9th Street told me how St. Paul's parishioners tended to be on the west side of 9th while Good Counsel's people were on the east side, across the street. These churches though, never posed as a source of conflict between the churchgoers. What is remarkable about 9th Street however, is that no one from St. Mary Magdalen's had a business there. Rarely did anyone from St. Mary's even shop around 9th Street by crossing 8th Street, I was told. Call it "church pride" but these churches were one of the few sources of identity in the new environment that an immigrant could have.

Regional Italian cuisines had not limited their uses of foodstuffs in the solid state especially in Philadelphia's ethnic communities where traditional "liquids" were manufactured for consumption. Take the case of Nazzareno Monticelli, the pharmacist and chemist who oriented his scientific skills towards the culinary arts at the 9th Street Market. Opening his store at 9th and Carpenter by 1900, Monticelli quickly became a name to all of Italian or Sicilian ancestry in the area. He was known for his "flavors." With his chemicals, Monticelli created a variety of tastes and aromas to flavor the clear, home-made alcohols into an "anisette," or a "scotch" or other fruitty or nutty spiked drinks.

Alcohol was not the only beneficiary of Monticelli's handiwork—the flavors were also used to enhance pastries and sometimes, meats. But, there was a much better alcohol for foods, such as meats. That is the all-time favorite—wine. Just when the making of wine within the neighborhood of "Little Italy" first occurred is an open question. Wine could be purchased in saloons and pubs as it had been since pre-Revolutionary times. But the "when" of wine-producing by native Italians and Sicilians in the Italian Market area is unknown. However, given that the making of wine requires some money to purchase the grapes and equipment and space to do it, the process itself would be outside the confines of the lifestyle of the average immigrant in the late nineteenth century.

So it was feasible for Nicola ("Nick") Marella in about 1904 to begin to import wine grapes for those with years of settlement, some financial grounding and time to be spent to produce a product considered more of a luxury than a necessity in the U.S. environment. Nick Marella was from Foggia but he is still remembered for his wine-grape business that began at 9th and Christian Streets and ended at 9th and Federal Streets. At the last location, he set up boxes atop boxes of the grapes in front of the Lafayette Cemetery, now Capitolo Playground. At one time, Nick had the same middleman-salesman who sold to Elmo Pio Wines in California, allow-ing the "average Joe" to make his home-made brew from the same grapes as the California wineries.

CHAPTER

South Ninth Street

as a

Marketplace & Social Scene

B Y 1915, THE AREA AROUND 9TH AND CHRISTIAN STREETS bore the "Italian Market" image despite the number of Eastern European Jews, African Americans, Irish Americans and other non-Italians who accented the neighborhood. The vestiges of the Farmers and Butchers Market from 8th and Christian oriented towards the west where movement continuously circulated between St. Paul's and Our Lady of Good Counsel Churches. It was at this time when the food market in and around South 9th Street began to gain public attention as one of Philadelphia's distinctive markets.

What may be the first publicity for Philadelphia's "Italian Market" appeared in *Travels in Philadelphia* after author Christopher Morley's visit before 1920. He still cited Christian Street near 9th as the place where "The Italian genius for good food" was found along with "Fish of every imaginable kind." He described the "pavement stalls of the little market" and the fact that locals "do not buy their food already prepared in cardboard boxes." It seemed that the "Italian Market" had finally come into its own by providing customers with the "fish, vegetables, cheeses, fruits and nuts...their chief delights."[32]

While more pushcarts were beginning to appear on the 900 and 1000 blocks of South 9th Street, the market on South 11th Street was still flourishing. After all, South 11th Street's broad central strip was planned long before the 9th Street Market. In fact, South 11th Street's market was much longer and wider than the usual city markets, running from, by some accounts, Bainbridge Street to Wharton.[33] It terminated near Moyamensing Prison.

The City of Philadelphia was compelled to build more neighborhood markets after the Consolidation Act in 1854 and the increase in migrations from abroad after the Civil War. The South 11th Street Market was originally a shed market in transition by the 1880s. Afterwards, either the sheds became dilapidated and were too expensive to replace or pushcart vending proved more economically efficient for the long stream of sheds to become the first in the city to be dismantled.[34]

By the 1920s, the South 11th Street Market began to appear more as the South 9th Street Market with curb-side vending. The produce introduced by Italians and Sicilians was their contribution to the U.S. diet. Whether on the movable pushcart or curbside stands, artichokes, endive, escarole, zucchini, dandelion (cicordia) and broccoli rabe were sold as "new" produce to Americans but were common to those in the peasant class abroad. In time, the demand for these veg-

Not a marketplace yet in 1905, but the pushcarts slowly begin to line up in front of some stores.

(photo by Brocato)

etables grew to such that farms in New Jersey and in Philadelphia's suburbs came to provide what importation was too costly or too tardy to do.

Backyard gardens, created by what vacant space was not part of the row-house, grew some favorites from the Mediterranean, and neighborhood residents used local resources to grow produce from the earth or vines or trees. Mr. Louis Sarcone, Sr. mused over memories of the 1920s and 1930s when Philadelphia's mounted police officers rode through "Little Italy" leaving mass amounts of "fertilizer" to those who followed the horses to the stables. Mr. Sarcone characterized this as a routine by those who prized their ancestors' legacy of handling the earth delicately so that it would yield treasures to the taste.

The Italian Market neighbors provided these vegetable dishes using traditional family recipes.

DOLORES ALVINI'S NEAPOLITAN BEAN SALAD

1 can (16 oz.) black beans ("I use the Goya.")

1 can (16 oz.) red kidney beans   1 can ceci pea

2 C   each: red onions and celery   1/4 C   olive oil

1/3 C   red wine vinegar   salt & pepper to taste

1/2 C red pepper, diced in tiny pieces

"'Empty beans into colander and rinse thoroughly under cold water. Place into a large bowl. Add the onions and celery." Pour in the olive oil, vinegar and season to taste. "Toss well and refrigerate. I always prepare this the day before needed.'"

FRANKIE PERRI'S BROCCOLI RABE CALABRESE

2 lbs. broccoli rabe   blended oil

"pinch of salt & pepper to taste"

3 T   garlic, "'chopped—I wouldn't dice it."

"Clean and sauté it up with hot seed pepper" added into the garlic and oil. "Let it disperse—I don't believe in cooking with salt." That's it!

The DiBruno's House of Cheese gang relinquished these delightful Abruzzese vegetable dishes:

BROCCOLI AND RIGATONI

8 T   olive oil   2 T   butter

4   cloves, garlic, minced   1 bunch broccoli, broken into florets

1C   chicken broth   1 lb.   rigatoni, cooked and drained

1 C   fresh basil, chopped   freshly grated romano or parmesan

1/4 C   fresh parsley, chopped

"In a large skillet, heat the oil and butter. Gently brown the garlic and broccoli and stir. Add the chicken broth. Cover and bring to a boil. Simmer until the broccoli is *al dente*. Add half of the basil and the rigatoni to the skillet. Mix together. Place in a heated serving dish. top with the parsley, pepper and cheese and remaining basil."

For four.

FRIED CAULIFLOWER

1 head, cauliflower	2 eggs
salt & pepper	1/2 C parmesan cheese
1 C flour, or more	seasoned Italian bread crumbs

"Partly boil the cauliflower. Break into pieces. Beat the eggs with the cheese, salt and pepper. Flour the cauliflower, dip in the egg mixture and then in bread crumbs. Fry in oil." Drain on a paper towel, then serve.

Makes about 4 servings.

STRING BEANS a la DiBRUNO

1 lb. string beans	1/2 C parmesan cheese
2 large cloves, garlic	2 large bay leaves
olive oil	salt & pepper
seasoned bread crumbs with cheese	almond slivers

"Sauté string beans in oil, salt, pepper, garlic and bay leaves. Add water to cover the beans. Let them cook. When the beans are cooked, add the bread crumbs and cheese."

Serves four as a side dish.

ESCAROLE & WHITE KIDNEY BEANS DiBRUNO

2 lbs. escarole	3 T olive oil
3 cloves garlic, chopped	1 can kidney beans (drained)
1 C chicken stock	hot pepper seeds, optional
salt & pepper	

"Wash and blanch the escarole. In a large sauce pan, pour the olive oil and add the chopped garlic. Salt and pepper to taste. Sauté the garlic until golden brown. Add to the escarole the kidney beans that were rinsed and blend. Add the chicken stock and let simmer for 30 minutes or until tender. Add the hot pepper seeds, if preferred."

The intersection of 9th and Christian Streets was a very noisy one indeed to imagine. The cries of hucksters moving about was bilingual in this area, though, unlike the strictly English hawkings heard uptown by the chimney sweeps, soft-soap seller and pepper pot vendors.[35] Movements by hundreds of people every hour and the clamor to buy this and buy that made this area between two Catholic churches very exciting in the 1920s.

Now, add to this atmosphere a damper to reality: where there is commerce, there is crime. In the many examples set by the immigrants towards working hard and saving diligently, there were always the possibilities of loss. But hardly anyone would guess that in the struggle in the quest to become an American that within the immigrant colony would exist those with other intentions. Merchants at the 9th Street Market were especially vulnerable to victimization. Those businessmen who owned real estate were very often the primary victims of the dreaded gang called the "Black Hand." These men were mostly of Neapolitan ancestry who could be criminally identified as extortionists, con-artists and thieves.[36] They made most of their incomes by threats to store owners in the form of harassment to customers or with damage to the stores.

One butcher whom I interviewed was still able to recall an encounter with a Black Hander. After over seventy years, the memory of the meeting still brought chills. Store fronts used to be bombed out because the owners refused to give the shake-down men any money. Black Handers used dynamite sticks everywhere around South 9th Street as well as on Christian Street to shatter doorways and dreams, to ruin reputations and to destroy confidence in the land of so many opportunities. Domenic Fante, Sr. took ill and died in 1922 as he was en route to report one such extortionist to the Postmaster General.[37] A few years later in his grocery store on 9th Street, the public read about Joseph Maggio's defense against an extortionist who got what was in Maggio's 12-gauge shot gun instead of what was in his cash register.[38] As another well-known 9th Street businessman said of the Camorra, another group of Neapolitans who shook-down 9th Streeters, fire was also a threat if $200.00 or $300.00 was not forthcoming to the gangsters.[39]

In time, as Black Hand aggression lessened on South 9th and Christian Street, more businesses opened because of a group known as "the Sicilians." If a store owner had a problem, he was told to see one of these "Sicilians" who were from western Sicily and were not afraid to counter the Neapolitan Black Handers.[40] Some store owners were able to pay for protection. But for those who struggled to make a living, "The Sicilians" understood. "...if you're an honest businessman, the Mafia won't bother you," said one 9th Streeter of market life with the gangsters.[41]

Yet, if any of these "Sicilians" ever died, the South 9th Street Market mourned as well by closing their shops and hanging black outside to express their condolences.[42] It was a simple way to acknowledge the men who protected Italian Market merchants, the providers of food, a basic need for the living.

❦

By the 1920s, one saw live animals in make-shift pens on South 9th Street, awaiting slaughter. This was called, "fresh" to butchers' customers. Lambs and goats, along with rabbits, fowl and many small "critter-like" animals were displayed for selection.

A customer makes a choice.

The animal is prepared to be food.

In the 19th century, lamb and mutton were popular U.S. dishes. For immigrants in Philadelphia's ethnic neighborhoods however, lamb was found on the tables of the Eastern European Jews, Lebanese and those from mainland Italy or Sicily who valued a more religious as well as traditional use for the meat. Lamb in the Italian Market area is prepared a few different ways. Here are some suggestions:

"GREEK-STYLE" LAMB
from George Vellios, via his grandmother.

5-6 lb. leg or shoulder of lamb	3-4 T oregano
salt & pepper to taste	4 cloves, garlic, chopped

Rinse the meat and cut small slits around the leg in which to insert the garlic pieces. Rub the meat with the oregano, salt and pepper and cover before placing in a preheated oven at 350°F for about 3 hours.

"There's not much to it!" said George. But this is good.

VIC POSPISCHIL'S ROAST LEG OF LAMB—ITALIAN-STYLE

(Shh! Vic learned to cook from his Italian wife and in-laws, plus what he's learned by working on 9th Street for so long.)

This recipe calls for a roasting pan with a rack.

6 lb.	leg of lamb	3-4	cloves, garlic, chopped
1 T	lemon peel	1/3 C	olive oil
1¹/₂ t	salt	1 t	rosemary
1 t	pepper	6-7	leaves, fresh basil or 1 t dry basil
1 t	adobo		

"Remove the kernel from the leg of lamb or any excessive fat or skin. Cut small slits in 5 or 6 areas on leg. In each slit, place a slice of garlic.

"Place the leg of lamb, skin-side down on rack in the pan. Insert a roast meat thermometer in the center of the thickest part of the leg, making sure that the bulb does not rest on the bone or in the fat.

"Sprinkle the leg with the lemon peel; then brush the meat with the olive oil. Then, combine and sprinkle over the meat the salt, pepper and rosemary." Add the remaining spices.

"Roast uncovered at 300°F for about 3¹/₂ hours for 30 to 35 minutes per pound. The meat is medium done when the thermometer is 175°F, or well done at 180°F.

"You can also baste the leg with a little of red wine after baking for about 2¹/₂ hours."

"This leg will give about 10 servings. Bon Appetit!"

Roseann Gugliuzzo Anthony's family has been scattered all over the 9th Street Market for decades. Her Grandpop DeMarco sold parsley on a stand. Only parsley. And he was able to provide for a large family by just selling the parsley. Other family members had stores and stands stretching over the blocks.

Roseann married a neighborhood boy who was of Lebanese ancestry. His mother taught Roe how to make this recipe with lamb.

ROSEANN GUGLIUZZO ANTHONY'S GRAPE LEAVES

Makes about fifty (50) or more finger-sized stuffed grape leaves.

1 large jar (about 32 oz.) grape leaves

Stuffing:

1 C white rice, cooked	1/2 C butter
11/2 lbs. of ground lamb	1/2 C lemon juice
garlic cloves ("lots!")	salt & pepper

"Put the stuffing in the grape leaves and roll them. When this is completed, put the grape leaves in a round pot in a circle. After every layer, put two cloves of sliced garlic." When completed, do another layer and continue with the sliced garlic.

"Add water to the pan and pour the butter with some salt on top and let it cook for 45 minutes on medium heat."

After this, "add one half of the lemon juice and put on a low fire. Cover the pot and cook for another 15 minutes. Then shut off heat and let the water evaporate."

<hr>

Prohibition at the Italian Market!

A twinkle in the eye and a look to repress a smile comes to the face of one former bootlegger named, Harry, when asked to recall alcohol vending at the Market. South 9th Street was no different than other places that made liquor. Harry said that he used molasses because it was less expensive than sugar to make an alcohol that could reach 200% proof. The clear brew was then "cut" with water to reduce the potency to a less hazardous drink. Bright colors, or hues like caramel were used in the bottles where the Monticelli "scotch" or "whiskey" flavors feigned the real.

But how accessible was this "hooch" in the neighborhood? Most local bootleggers used legitimate stores, like the *gelaterie* (ice cream shops), *pasticcerie* (pastry shops) or *café* (coffee shops) as fronts for selling alcohol.[43] But the men would probably rather term this practice as "hospitality" to those who used to frequent the bars and saloons that were subject to the Volstead Act. A shot of "whiskey" in the coffee. Or some "anisette" with a few cookies. Some peppery *taralli* with some "scotch." These were the typical repasts.

Nicola Matarazzo's pastry shop on the 800 block of Christian Street also sold ice cream to "Little Italy" shoppers around the turn of the 20th century.

The 800 block of Christian Street had the most pastry shops in the area by the 1920s. The "other use" for sugar and molasses had a more widespread and legitimate consumption by people of all religious, ethnic and racial groups. Even the Temperance suffragists could not argue about pastries! In Philadelphia's "Little Italy," one's sweet tooth could rot with the selection of artistic delights that too often were too beautiful to eat.

Some of the following recipes are well known here, but require a personal touch by the baker. These are for the creative!

VERSATILE SPONGE CAKE

4 C	flour (self-rising is good)	3 t	baking powder
8	eggs	1½ C	sugar
2	sticks softened butter or margarine	2 t	vanilla

Cream the sugar with butter or margarine, then gradually add the other ingredients and mix to consistency. Pour this into a greased and floured cake pan and bake in a pre-heated oven at 350°F for 30 to 45 minutes or until a knife comes out clean when inserted.

Artificial rum flavor can be used after the cake is baked and cooled. Soak the cake with the rum, add Dr. LoBianco's cream filling recipe and ice. A Sicilian Cassata!

THE LaTERZA FAMILY'S ITALIAN WEDDING COOKIES

6 large eggs, lightly beaten		1 C	sugar
1 C	olive oil	1 t	vanilla extract
6 t	baking powder	4 C	flour

On a tabletop or board, make a well with the 2 C of flour. Add the sugar, olive oil, vanilla and baking powder. Gradually add the eggs, mixing them with your fingers until a soft dough forms

Drop teaspoonfuls of the dough onto an ungreased cookie sheet about 2" apart. Bake at 350°F in a preheated oven for about 10 mins. or until cookies are lightly browned. When cooled, use this:

Traditional icing: 1/2 lb. confectioners' sugar 2 t lemon extract and water on the side.

Combine all of these ingredients until smooth. Add more water if too dry. Try some sugar sprinkles on top for more color.

Another favorite made at LoBianco's Bakery, a simpler version:

TORRONE

2 C	whole almonds and 1 C hazelnuts, both roasted		
2 C	sugar	2	egg whites
1 C	corn syrup	2 t	vanilla
1/4-1/3 water		1	stick soft butter or margarine
pinch of salt			

On medium heat, mix sugar, corn syrup, salt and water until consistent and smooth. In separate bowl, with mixer, beat egg whites to stiff peaks. Gradually pour 1/2 sugar mixture into egg whites and continue to beat. Bring to higher heat (250°F, not higher) the sugar mixture; then add this to bowl mix and stir in remaining ingredients except the nuts. When consistent, add nuts by hand.

Pour into buttered pan or baking dish and even out the batter to dry as is. Refrigerate for 2 or more hours until hardened. Then cut into bite-size pieces.

Yields about 2 lbs.

BASIC ITALIAN COOKIE DOUGH

3 1/2 C all-purpose flour		2	eggs
1 t	baking soda	1	stick butter or margarine, softened
1/2 C	sugar	1 t	vanilla
pinch of salt		1 t	almond extract

With mixer, cream sugar with butter or margarine and gradually add the other ingredients to form a soft dough. Chill dough in the refrigerator for about 3 hours or until it is more durable. One can also spoon softened dough onto greased and floured cookie pan and fill with nuts, maraschino cherries or fruit preserves. Or add chocolate chips or chopped nuts. Or put soft dough into a pastry bag and shoot out different cookie shapes. Or drizzle with chocolate. Or ice, or sprinkle with jimmies, or shake on confectioners' sugar.

If there was a "Golden Age" in the history of the 9th Street "Italian Market," it was in the 1920s through the 1940s. This ever-changing neighborhood and Market spirited through a glorious Prohibition, a Depression felt by a few and a world war that reminded locals of patriotism solely to the United States of America.

The South 9th Street Market was part of a crowded community in the 1930s with over forty religious at St. Paul's, over twenty nuns and priests at Good Counsel and more than a dozen at St. Mary Magdalen's, along with the Presbyterian, Baptist, Episcopal ministers and quite a few rabbis living there.[44] Area public schools were as full as the Catholic schools with the children coming from the same ethnic and economic backgrounds.

Lifestyles were comparatively similar within the neighborhood, with most, but not all, people eating the same. At the close of each shopping day, those who faced the worst adversities, usually elderly women, would converge on 9th Street to try to buy what could not be sold the next day. Abject poverty as well as the good life, (exemplified sometimes by hostesses who used the paper doilies for house guests), exposed the extremes of the economic classes in this South Philadelphia community.

The early 1930s was the time when the steak sandwich was created by Pasquale "Pat" Olivieri.[45] Tired of eating hot dogs, he suggested frying thinly sliced beef with onions, then loading it in a small loaf of Italian bread. This however, does not mean the beginning of the American fast food culture! Here, as in other cities in the U.S., the hot dog and other sandwiches were popular. In Philadelphia's "Little Italy," the more common sandwiches were pepper and eggs, baloney and eggs, any meat with cheese, tomato and lettuce that was "hoagie-like" and sandwiches made of roasted pork or beef. One George Vellios, sold "sandwiches" at 9th and Christian Streets that only had meat drippings inside!

Approaching the 1940s and a war that would have limitless influences, the Market that now flourished on South 9th Street between Christian and Wharton Streets established a name for itself as a mecca for bargains. Large families were especially attracted to a place where food was seemingly ubiquitous. There was no food that could not be purchased there—the Market had everything! Even if one had little or no money for food, a butcher would give out scraps or bones that would otherwise be put into the garbage can. Some people still remember the times, pre-Social Security, when the damaged goods were all one could afford.

Those were the days when...

> *The pavements were not deep enough to hold the density of shoppers;*
>
> *The demands were too often greater than the supplies;*
>
> *and, what's this? Horsemeat!*

Things happen, even in times when a "Golden Age" on 9th Street wanes because of wartime restrictions. Food coupon fraud, violating the rationing allowed and substituting one meat for, well, something meat-like and edible were the covert reasons why some businesses at the Market have been able to survive today. These were times when on-site slaughtering was commonplace on 9th Street, when produce was purchased from railroad cars nearby and carted to the Market and when 9th Street was able to provide neighborhood residents with everything from girdles to piano rolls to feathers to pliers.

One 9th Streeter, Vincent "Babe" Barbadoro, poetically recalled Christmas time shopping at the Italian Market during the 1950s:

> *I remember walking with my mother*
> *Trying not to get lost through a forest of legs.*
> *Boots, coats, gloves—into the cold we would ascend,*
> *Oh, yes, we also wore our leggings back then!*
>
> *Vendors selling from stores and stands—*
> *They yelled, "we have celery, fish and potatoes!*
> *Yo! You! Don't squeeze the tomatoes!"*
>
> *Yes, the vendor was like a magic man:*
> *Risking the flames from the fire can.*
> *Brown bags full, hanging from my hands;*
> *I did it as a youth*
> *Now, I do it as a man.*

The post-war period brought the local residents more in touch with the outside world through more foods. Forget about sacrificing oneself and one's family on one *minestra* after another! The period after the Second World War heralded prosperity and a tendency to spend more on foods usually purchased for special times. Some Italian Market merchants also took to utilizing the "conveniences" only found on 9th Street such as the fire barrels where "Roe Roe" Lombardo and Anthony Scali found culinary purposes, the awnings for hanging peppers to dry and the "open refrigeration" at the stands where Mr. Flocco (alias "Gump") managed to keep without fear of theft.

Now, our Italian Market can handle requests from around the world and is able to service the most difficult-to-find foodstuffs. The Market's ethnic composition has gone through the same cycles of immigrants as in other East Coast cities, yet has maintained more of the early twentieth century's business character. The Eastern European Jewish contingent is still in proportion to those of Italian and Sicilian ancestries with the Evantashes' and Redels' stores run by the third generations. *The Philadelphia Inquirer*'s Tom Ferrick, Jr. estimated that about one-third of 9th Street's businesses have owners of Asian descent. The blacks from the Caribbean and continental Africa with Orlando Muñiz's Latin foods also add their

Rocco Turra at his stand at 9th Street and Washington Avenue in 1959, wearing a smile and earrings of cherries.

(Urban Archives. Temple University.)

flavors to this street where camaraderie is very evident with the music, the smiles and the kinder versions of "don't touch!"

A visitor to this neighborhood sees what the nineteenth century urban expansion introduced as well as left in its architecture. Commercially, the latest technology connects the 9th Street Italian Market to nations far and away. Yet, there are many who still are content here with the fire barrels for heat and who are able to earn substantial incomes in the food industry without much education. Esposito's Meats, founded in 1911 is still here and so (occasionally!) is Herbie Green and "Irv's" and the street number.

Ah, what memories! Rossano's is gone as are the butcher who made chicken taste like pheasant (and sold it as pheasant), the glistening fabrics of Max Wilk & Daughter's, the coal yard, the cops who got the freebies, Benny Strano, the "Chinese Cemetery," the gypsy boy and the woman who threw her husband out of a window.

But then, gone too are the signs on at least half of the businesses on the street!

The purpose of this book was to record the history of one of Philadelphia's most popular sites, an enchanting neighborhood of heroes and monsters, wonder and awe, able to transform its residents into more than incredible characters. Here is a Philadelphia community that is worth more than a glance as one rides through the streets.

The ghosts of those who grieved the hard times of the past can still be felt.

Restless energy is alive everywhere, searching to settle.

Look beyond what may seem to be disorganized because it has been here for awhile now.

Sit down and eat something.

Or just digest what you now know about Philadelphia's Italian Market and the tastes of South Ninth Street.

ENDNOTES

1. JULIANI, RICHARD N. *Building Little Italy.* University Park, PA: Penn State University Press, 1998. pp. xv,1-49; also refer to Dr. Juliani's chart on p. 147.

2. Ibid., pp. 3; 32; 51.

3. Ibid., pp. 28-29.

4. Ibid., especially Chapters 1 through 3.

5. Ibid. Juliani showed demographic dispersions throughout the book, but for the settlement of a "Little Italy" that remained more static than other temporary Italian colonies in Philadelphia, refer to pp. 198-321.

6. *The Catholic Herald*, published in Philadelphia on July 22, 1852.

7. Ibid.

8. The major Philadelphia newspapers were particularly critical of the Irish in the 1830s and 1840s. A very good source of Irish crime in South Philadelphia (i.e., south of South Street) is found in DAVID JOHNSON'S *Policing the Urban Underworld—The Impact of Crime on the Development of the American Police, 1800 to 1887.* Philadelphia: Temple U. Press, 1979.

9. Oral histories taken from 1992 to present.

10. Gopsill's Philadelphia City Directory for 1885. Published by James Gopsill in Philadelphia in 1886.

11. Ibid.

12. Some later accounts which documented the history of markets and those in transition are: WALTHER, RUDOLPH J. *Happenings in Ye Olde Philadelphia, 1680-1900.* Phila.: 1925, pp. 174-176, and JACKSON, JOSEPH. *Encyclopedia of Philadelphia.* Harrisburg, PA: Telegraph Press, 1931, pp.535; 875-876.

13. Gopsill's City Directory of 1888.

14. Ibid.

15. Interview of Mr. Luke Marano taken in 1998.

16. Gopsill's City Directory of 1888.

17. Ibid.

18. Enumeration Lists of the 1900 Census for the City and County of Philadelphia, Roll 1452, Nos. 50 to 53. National Archives, Philadelphia, PA.

19. Gopsills' City Directory of 1897, p. 2248.

20. Ibid.

21. Interview with Mr. James Tayoun in 1998.

22. Enumeration Lists of 1900, op. cit.

23. Ibid.

24. Ibid.

25. Ibid.

26. According to the writer of *La Colonia di Filadelfia*. Published by L'Opinione in Philadelphia in 1906.

27. Ibid.

28. The Catholic Directory and the Archdiocese of Philadelphia's Catholic Charities and Social Welfare Activities, Published in Philadelphia in 1922.

29. Records of the Missionary Sisters of the Third Order of St. Francis, Peeksill, New York.

30. The Catholic Directories of 1905-07.

31. Various oral histories and interviews taken from 1992 to present.

32. MORLEY, CHRISTOPHER. *Travels in Philadelphia*. Philadelphia: J.B. Lippincott Co., 1920. pp. 17-20.

33. There is some confusion with Jackson's sources: on p. 876 he refers to the "Shed Market" on South Eleventh Street, from "Bainbridge to Catharine Streets" then, to the "Curb Market" on South Eleventh Street, "Between Christian and Wharton Streets", (p. 535).

34. Ibid., p. 876.

35. SCARF & WESTCOTT. *History of Philadelphia*. Philadelphia: Edwin S. Stuart Publishing, 1884, as cited in Jackson, op. cit., p. 535.

36. Oral histories and interviews of victims of the Black Hand in Philadelphia and in suburbs.

37. Oral history taken by Mary Rose Cunningham Fante of her uncle, Dominic Fante.

38. Local newspapers and the Philadelphia Police's Homicide Records.

39. Oral history of Dominic Fante, op. cit.

40. Numerous interviews taken from 1992 to present.

41. Oral history of Dominic Fante, op. cit.

42. Oral history.

43. Oral histories and interviews from 1993-1994.

44. The Catholic Directories of 1920 and 1930. The City Directories.

45. This common belief has become fact.

PART 2

THE TASTES
OF THE
SOUTH 9TH STREET
ITALIAN MARKET

To know a good piece of meat or produce from a bad one is not essential when shopping at the South 9th Street "Italian Market." Instead, bring a sense of humor and an open mind, and be prepared for the unconventional. It will be an uncommon shopping experience to say the least!

This neighborhood has always had quite a reputation!

The Native Americans called the area of which the Italian Market is part, "The place of pigeon droppings." Sure, it was a fertile here: when groups of British and Irish ancestries lived here in the 19th century, the neighborhood's reputation for violence was impressionable to the historians who recorded hardly anything good about the area but for the arsons, extortions, piracy and armed conflicts between the legendary gangs. This was pre-"Little Italy."

Since then, the people who are of the Market neighborhood add the ingredients for a local food history and culture. A little of salt and pepper here, a little bit of basil there. Maybe something sweet in-between to cleanse the palate—the people at, in, around and from the 9th Street "Italian Market" will give some "tasteful" accounts on life in the neighborhood from throughout this century.

The photo on the previous page is of The Italian Market Festival in 1976. as seen from 800 block South 9th Street. **Everybody Loves 9th Street.**

(Photo courtesy of Mr. Harry Crimi.)

DRESSING ON SOUTH 9TH STREET

Begin your cultural journey in the Italian Market at Sarcone's where the warmth stays within the Sarcone family and employees after the breads have cooled.

It happened that a conversation begun in the store on the mal'occhio ("evil eye") suddenly is transformed from the incredible to the edible. Lovable Alfonso Meseté, the custodian at Sarcone's Bakery told a story of when his mother had the mal'occhio. In desperation, the poor woman went to the "mal'occhio-remover" who could make the headache, nausea, dizziness and other symptoms disappear with the prayers, gestures and other voodoo-like apparatus.

"Ma! What happened?" Al asked his mother. "Ma! You smell like a salad!" He told us that his poor suffering mother had "oil, oregano, salt"...whatever... rubbed on her as if she was a piece of lettuce. But the best part was, (no, not the tomato!) that she was mal'cchio-free!

Emilio ("Meemee") Mignucci, the only alumnus of The Restaurant School at the Italian Market and owner of DiBruno's House of Cheese created this basic Italian salad dressing:

EMILIO'S VINEGARETTE

3/4 C	" good extra virgin olive oil"	pinch of dry oregano
1/4 C	balsamic vinegar ("or better, sherry")	pinch of dry basil
1 t	chopped garlic	salt & pepper to taste

748 SOUTH 9TH STREET

What's old is new at Sarcone's Bakery.

In the store's beginning, after over a decade of Italian bread-making, Lou Sarcone tried "American" bread. It was sliced too, just like the other American breads. A steady clientele wanted it, but in time, Italian breadmaking became the only product in which Sarcone's based their fine reputation. No one missed their sliced American bread. Everybody preferred the Italian, seeded or not.

Sarcone's outlasted more than one-half dozen bread bakeries within one block of their store. "Anyone with an oven in their cellar made bread," said Mr. Louis Sarcone. He remembered pizza sold at the store begun by his grandfather in 1911. His grandmother, Rosina, made an unforgetable pizza for sale and for the family.

ROSINA'S PIZZA

1 prepared pizza shell	3 to 4 medium onions (or more, if desired)
3 T cooking oil	course black pepper

Sauté onions in frying pan with oil and coarse black pepper. Spread onions over pizza shell and bake in oven until shell is cooked through. Optional: salt and more coarse pepper. One can also drip olive oil on top for a moister pizza.

WAS AT 813 SOUTH 9TH STREET

Attorney Gustine Pelagatti presented a "case scenario":

"Suppose that I establish a place like the '40s and '50s where people, ordinary people, could eat affordable food."

The Jury nodded in agreement.

"And suppose that I have at this established place some basic southern Italian and Abruzzese cuisine, like bracciole, beans and greens..."

The people in the courtroom sigh: "Ah-h-h!"

"...meatballs and macaroni..."

"Yes! Yes!"

"Escarole Soup!"

"Ooh-ooh! Yes!"

The rise in emotions made the Judge strike his gavel: "Order! Order!"

"Yes, Your Honor, let's order!"

Mr. Pelagatti and his friend, Frank Palumbo, Sr. bought Mike D'Alfonso's old funeral home, renovated the front room to be a dining room and the embalming room became the kitchen. "I named it 'The Nostalgia,' " said Mr. Pelagatti. "Palumbo's" was primarily a catering establishment for private gatherings; Frank, Sr. loved Pelagatti's idea of a public restaurant which would serve the Abruzzese food of their heritage. Oh, how many people came to "The Nostalgia" and felt guilty about all they ate! It was almost criminal!

But it was worth it!

Mr. Pelagatti shares "Pasta Bolognese," as served in "Nostalgia."

PASTA BOLOGNESE

3 T	olive oil	3 lbs.	pork, veal & beef, chopped
2	cloves garlic, diced	1 T	salt
1 t	sugar	1 T	oregano
1	green pepper, diced	1 T	basil
1	small onion, diced	1 T	Italian seasoning
1	(16 oz.) can crushed tomatoes	1	(8 oz.) can salsa
16 oz.	water		

"In a dutch oven or deep pot, sauté onion and garlic with oil until golden. Then add rest of ingredients over medium heat and stir until meat is cooked through. Then, add tomatoes, salsa and water. Simmer for about 1 hour over low heat. Serve over short, cut macaroni, like ziti, ragatoni or even bow ties and wagon wheels."

WAS AT 813 SOUTH 9TH STREET

Frank Palumbo once claimed to have owned the largest bar in the world: it sat over 2,000 patrons. But that was at Fifteenth and Market Streets in Center City. At "Palumbo's," his bar/restaurant/night club, Frank treated politicians, celebrities and even orphans all to the same courtesies as he would to the paying public.

He was an extraordinary individual.

"Palumbo's" extended from Darien to 9th Street at Catharine Street and represented the hospitality and warmth of the Market neighborhood.

Frank's beautiful wife, Kippee gives her recipe for "Chicken Rosemary" which she used to make for her celebrity guests at her home. "They just flipped for it." We will too.

KIPPEE PALUMBO'S CHICKEN ROSEMARY

Makes four servings.

4	large breasts or 4 whole legs of chicken	1/4 C	crushed rosemary
1	stick butter or 1/4 C oil	salt & pepper to taste	
2	whole cooking onions		

Kippee said to get a big baking or pan and place washed and dried chicken which has been rubbed on both sides with the salt/pepper mix in it.

Then, lay some butter or put some oil atop each piece of chicken. Place onions in pan. Sprinkle chicken with crushed rosemary and cover pan with aluminum foil. Bake in pre-heated oven for about 1 ½ hours at 350°F. Kippee recommends to cover the chicken for one-half the time, then leave the chicken uncovered *on broil* for the last five minutes of cooking. You can add potatoes in with the chicken and onions. In-between cooking time, baste the chicken with the drippings for a more moist taste.

Kippee's recipe calls for the skin to be left on the chicken; it will turn crisp with this recipe. The skin can also be removed prior to the baking and broiling.

WAS AT 822 SOUTH 9TH STREET

Retired gynecologist and obstetrician Salvatore J. Cucinotta, MD, born in 1910, recalled his adolescence during Prohibition when the Lanzetti brothers and other local gangsters made the intersection of 9th and Christian Streets appear as Swiss cheese with their gun battles. Bullets pierced through many a building there.

Antonio "Nino the Boat" Cucinotta's grocery store at 822 South 9th Street had to replace its front windows several times a month because of the stray bullets from the gangsters who shot from passing cars, rooftops or on foot. Enroute to school at Our Lady of Good Counsel School, little Salvatore Cucinotta literally learned to dodge bullets sometimes. Eventually, Dr. Cucinotta grew so accustomed to the shoot-outs that when he was in battle in World War II, he remained fearless in gunfire, again dodging the bullets. "A piece of cake!"

One of the chief products sold at Cucinotta's Grocery was Pop's home-made ricotta. Accordingly, here's a recipe for ricotta cake:

RICOTTA CAKE

2¼ lbs	ricotta cheese	6	eggs
1 C	sugar	6 T	flour
1 t	vanilla extract	1 t	each: orange , lemon zest;
16 oz.	cream cheese		white raisins, citron and
1 pt.	sour cream		almonds or pine nuts

Preheat oven to 350° F. Combine all ingredients in bowl and mix to consistency. Place in a greased and floured spring pan or Bundt-type of cake pan. Bake for 45 mins. to l hour or until top of cake is cracked. Cool before serving.

Beware: this is a very rich cake!

Note: Dr. Cucinotta's son, Attorney Salvatore, Jr. remembers that his family was also known for putting sugar in the ricotta filling of their ravioli.

WAS AT 823 SOUTH 9TH STREET

Mr. Anthony Lucchesi just sometimes recalls how his father, Salvatore's fish business was able to survive ninety-seven(97) years on 9th Street. They did well until he had to close the shop in 1998. It broke his heart to do so.

Lucchesi's fish store's success brought the Anastasios, Michalis and Darigos from Spadafora, Sicily to sell fish on 9th Street when competition wasn't even an issue with the tens of thousands frequenting the Market each week. Those were the days when walking the 9th Street Market was slowed by the thickness of the crowds each day, not just on weekends.

The Lucchesi family ate what they sold and no one was tired of fish. Ever. Mary Lucchesi, "my mother was one terrific cook," said her son. What did she make with fish? Mr. Lucchesi remembered when his brother, Dr. Pat, brought home a colleague. It was Friday and Mrs. Lucchesi had macaroni and "meatballs." The dinner guest, a non-Catholic, questioned eating meat on Friday. "It wasn't meat. But the way my mother made 'em, they tasted like meatballs," added Mr. Lucchesi, wistfully. Mary Lucchesi made meatballs of tuna. In the tomato gravy, there's a tasty exchange of flavors.

"I miss my mother's cooking. It was so good."

MARY LUCCHESI'S TUNA BALLS

6 cans (6 oz.) tuna in water, drained or 2¼ lbs. fresh tuna, filleted

4	eggs		
½ C	diced onion	¼ C	parsley
2 C	bread crumbs	salt and pepper to taste	

Mix all of the ingredients together and form into 2" balls. Place in frying pan with oil; or boil in water; or bake in oven until half cooked. Then place the tuna balls in tomato gravy and continue to cook until tuna balls are finished.

Serve and eat as meatballs, with macaroni or in an Italian roll.

This recipe should make about 10 to 12 tuna balls.

827 SOUTH 9TH STREET

The oldest person on 9th Street passed on to a better place during the course of this book. Angelina Bosconti LaRosa, a beautiful woman who was born in 1901 and who almost lived to see the next century is remembered as possibly the person who shopped the longest at the Italian Market. Her motto could have been,

"Eat Longer—Buy Food at 9th Street" but this lady, who would never leave her home without high heels and pretty dress made dishes that her daughters and granddaughters now revere.

Angelina was born in Belmonte, outside of Palermo, Sicily and had ten children with her husband, John. Her daughter, Rosalie called her mother's cooking, "gourmet ... the merchants in the Italian Market will remember her for buying the best and freshest vegetables." Another talent of hers was her sewing. Would you believe that Angelina made the Holy Communion outfits for her eldest four children from her wedding gown? And she managed this while taking in tailoring work for Jacob Reeds.

Angelina's girls parted with one of their mother's dishes that is typically Palermitano:

ANGELINA LaROSA'S PASTA WITH CAULIFLOWER

1	packet of saffron	1	large cauliflower
1	large onion	1 lb.	short macaroni of choice
3 T	olive oil + 2 T more	1	small clove garlic, chopped
1 C	Italian-flavored bread crumbs	1 C	grated locatelli cheese

salt & pepper to taste

"Wash and pull apart the cauliflower into small pieces. In a deep skillet over medium heat, sauté olive oil with onion and garlic. Gradually add the cauliflower with the packet of saffron that was diluted in 1 C water. Add another cut of water and the salt and pepper. Cook on medium heat for about 15 minutes or until the cauliflower is soft. Everything should be a yellowish color. Add more water to make a nice sauce.

"While cooking the cauliflower in the skillet, on another burner boil the macaroni until it is done. Drain water from this pot, leaving the macaroni. Pour the cauliflower mix over the macaroni and mix together. In another skillet, sauté the breadcrumbs in 2 T olive oil. Then toss this over the macaroni and cauliflower. Add the grated locatelli and serve."

Makes about 4 servings.

GUILTY OF SHOOT-OUTS AT 9TH & CHRISTIAN STREETS

The Lanzetti brothers were unquestionably the most publicity-seeking gangsters around the 9th Street Market in the 1920s and 1930s. The brothers were neither Black Handers nor Mafiosi but they nonetheless antagonized others in the underworld with their endless criminal activities.

Five of the six infamous Lanzetti brothers, as they appeared to law enforcement in the 1930s.

The Lanzettis loved to read about themselves in the newspapers and very often did things to keep Philadelphia's readers' attention. Their father started one of the first Italian restaurants in the city before 1900. But, the family thereafter struggled. The parents and children lived in several homes around the Market but failed to own any house or business for too long. The six Lanzetti sons, all gangsters, claimed that committing crime was the only way that they could eat.

It was probably this gang that brought organized illegal gambling to the neighborhood while Prohibition was still in effect. Not that these brothers and their fellow gangsters were not bootleggers too, but they got plenty of locals to play the numbers with them. Many stores on 9th Street did accept the bookmakers' requests to take the numbers from customers. And, of course, storeowners were duly compensated for this type of "side-job."

A good number to bet? Try the ever-popular: "4-4-4."

The street jargon for winning the number is "making a hit." If one did not "hit," then it was back to eating peppers and eggs!

PEPPERS & EGGS

1 lb. bell peppers (red or green) cut into 1" pieces

3 to 4 eggs, beaten with ½ C milk and, ⅓ C locatelli cheese (grated)

1 medium onion, diced

3 T oil

salt & pepper to taste

On medium heat, add oil to pan and then the peppers. Cook with the onion until tender. Add egg mixture and stir. Sprinkle with salt and pepper and serve while still warm.

Makes about 3 or 4 servings.

THE NAME THAT LIVES IN LIVER AT THE ITALIAN MARKET.

The name, "John Righi" is one destined to be remembered for extraordinary experiences.

It is the name of the father who at a very young age would yell, "Shopping bags!" on 9th Street, or give 10¢ pony rides to children at the Market. After eating 9th Street groceries for years, John Righi was hired to watch the stacked boxes of produce at night to prevent thefts at the Market.

We'd like to recall the name, "John Righi" as the proud owner of the old Columbus Hall, founded in 1867 which became "Mama Yolanda's Restaurant" and the name of the beloved son who as a chef prodigy kept Sammy Davis, Jr. coming back for more to eat.

The woman who named "John Righi" was indeed Mama Yolanda, a superb chef whose precocious grandson, John Righi, Jr. continued in her cooking tradition. Kim Righi Abdalla, Jr.'s sister, quickly recalled, "My brother was 14 years old when he cooked liver casaling' for Sammy Davis, Jr." John Jr. would repeat this recipe many times at Mama Yolanda's. In fact, everytime that Sammy was in town, John, Jr. made the entertainer only one dish, which Sammy wanted over and over. Here it is!

JOHN RIGHI'S LIVER CASALINGA

2	long strips, calves livers	2	green sweet peppers, cut
2	medium Spanish onions, sliced	1 C	white wine
1 C	any stock	1 T	butter
2-3	cloves, garlic, diced	2	strips of crispy bacon
2 T	olive oil	1 T	parsley
salt & pepper to taste		1/2 C	flour

"Flour liver and place in a saucepan with the olive oil. Brown on both sides. Drain off the olive oil, add the garlic and onions and peppers and sauté until garlic and onions are golden. Then add the stock, wine, salt and pepper and lastly, the butter. Arrange the bacon on top."

Serves one.

Recommended as sides, (as at "Mama Yolanda's"): "roasted potatoes or sautéed green beans."

KEPT ALIVE BY EATING 9TH STREET'S GOODIES?

"Mr. Migs" had several attempts on his life as a Mafioso in the U.S. but he dodged many bullets on the European battlefields too. A fixture at 8th and Christian Streets, "Mr. Migs" shopped at the Italian Market for his produce.

Then-President George Bush sent "Mr. Migs" a birthday card because he lived past one hundred years. Was it luck or his diet?

Maybe it was because "Mr. Migs" ate his vegetables!

This is one of his dishes from his native Sicily.

"'MR. MIGS' 'VEGETABLE MEDLEY'"

1 C	fava beans	1 (16 oz.) can cannelloni beans w/ water	
1 C	asparagus tips only	1/2 C	baby peas
2	cloves garlic, diced	2 T	olive oil
salt & pepper to taste			

Sauté garlic in hot oil until golden. Add the fava beans first and cook until tender. Then add the remaining ingredients. A creamy sauce will develop from the water and cannelloni beans. Season to taste and serve.

Makes about 4 to 6 portions.

WAS ON BEAT AT ITALIAN MARKET FOR 13 YEARS!

Thanks to over a century of bad press in the news media, Italians and Sicilians have been, too often, the subject of crime associated with these groups instead of a tribute to those who rescued western European cuisine with culinary expertise.

Checking any prospects of criminal activity at the Market is our affable bike cop, Patrolman Gil Bromley who in recent years has experienced an appetizing tour of duty as he rides past the visual, olfactory and, (can he help it?) taste sensations while watching for unnecessary traffic or an occasional theft. Prior to Officer Bromley were a few unforgetable of "Philly's Finest," like "Joe the Greaser," lovable Frank and of course, the now-retired no-nonsense Felix Tartaglia who added humor while enforcing the law.

Sure, Felix met many celebrities in his thirteen years at the Market. His captain, Thomas Nestel, wanted him to be known to everyone at the Market. "I have a lot of great memories from 9th Street. For me, it has a special meaning." He met Bill Cosby, Pat Cooper and David Brenner there but his most memorable experience was when he met Alexander Calder there. "He'd come into town. They were fêting him for his work but the food ran out. He then asked to go to 'Palumbo's' to eat." Calder did Felix's portrait, which may have been his last art work before he died.

Felix loves to cook and he's serious about what he does. He submitted this old, we mean old, recipe from his great-grandmother from Sicily...

FELIX THE COP'S GREAT-GRANDMOTHER'S "BIFSTECCA al POMODORO"

2 lbs.	thinly cut round steak	8 cloves garlic, diced	
2 cans (16 oz.) plum tomatoes		1 small can (3 oz.) tomato paste	
4	basil leaves	3 oz. red wine	
3 T	locatelli cheese (grated)	dash peppermint	
1/4 t	sugar	2 T olive oil	
oregano to taste			

"In a casserole dish or deep frying pan over medium heat, brown steak on both sides. Then add remaining ingredients to cook for 15 minutes over medium heat; then, another 10 minutes over lower heat.

"On side: Prepare 1 1/2 C long grain white rice as directed, and,
    "1 can (16 oz.) early June peas" ("They're a little sweeter.")

"To serve: Place rice on large dish, place peas on top, then spoon tomato and beef mixture last on top." Felix said to use some of the fresh peppermint or basil as a garnish.

Serves four.

WHOLESALE HONOR AND RESPECT

It is said that former Mafia boss Angelo Bruno had a grocery store at the 9th Street Market. He was just a regular guy back then who sold canned goods and had some items in big burlap sacks. One shopper to his store claimed that Bruno gave discounts on his products. He did have a way with numbers, no doubt about that. Bruno could apply his knowledge of economics to any business venture and succeed.

The Mafia boss who ran Philadelphia's Family for about twenty-one years had other grocery stores in South Philadelphia after this Italian Market store closed. And he did well with his stores, selling the imported Italian foodstuffs. But, as the saying goes, there were bigger and better things ahead, beyond Italian food.

Bruno was not too picky about what he ate, but, said his daughter, Jeanne, he liked his macaroni to "have a bite," not too *al dente.* A practical guy, Bruno gave no advice on cooking but did say, "Run the blade, dodge the bullet."

Oh, he also said to wash your hands after using the bathroom and before eating.

Nicky Cimino and Jeanne Bruno recalled this dish that Mr. B. liked alot.

"PASTA PATAT'"

3-4 large white Idaho potatoes	1 lb. linguini, prepared
tomato gravy, already prepared	½ C red wine

Nicky explained: "Part-boil the potatoes that have been cut into quarters (or bite-sized pieces). Add them to the gravy with a little red wine and water and let it cook for 5 to 10 minutes." Then, let the potatoes in gravy mix with the prepared, drained macaroni and serve.

Nicky said, "You gotta eat it fast—it will get thick" if left out too long, "but of course, no one here lets it sit!"

THE ALTERNATIVE TO "PALUMBO'S"

Marie Muscarelli Masi is Vito's wife and one of those rare cooks who could figure out how to prepare any cuisine, "Dutch, Polish, Italian...anything I cook. I cook everything." The first "Marie's Luncheonette" at 821 Catharine Street opened in 1936 with Mario Lanza who "used to deliver stuff." Jimmy Durante and "all the show people, like the dancers, musicians, anyone that went into 'Palumbo's,' hanged here with us," she said. "Them used to be the days." Working 6 A.M. past midnight, Marie? She didn't mind.

Marie was born in Naples in 1917 and came to Philadelphia in 1922. A self-taught cook, she learned to make veal scallopini, stuffed calamari, stuffed egg-plant and served her regulars, like Maggio's Cheese's workers, "around the big round table in the kitchen." Frequenting later at "Marie's Luncheonette" when it moved to 827 Christian Street was Chubby Checkers, who was then a worker at Tony Anastasio's Produce.

Marie's recipe is a crowd-pleaser like its creator!

MARIE'S STUFFED ARTICHOKES WITH SHRIMP

6	cloves, garlic, diced	1/2 C	grated pecorino romano
1/3 C	olive oil	1/4 C	Italian parsley
3 C	Italian bread crumbs	1 lb.	small shrimp
6	artichokes		chicken broth

"Cut off the stems at the bottoms of each artichoke. Then put each artichoke upside down and press it on a surface to loosen the leaves. Remove the pincers with scissors. Rinse the artichokes in cold water then stuff with the shrimp stuffing that follows.

"In a bowl, pour in the olive oil, add the bread crumbs and other ingredients and mix. Wet this mixture down with the chicken broth to form a soft dough. This is the stuffing.

"In a large, deep pot or Dutch oven, fill half of the pot with water and add the chopped garlic and salt to taste," or as Marie prefers, chicken stock/broth. She also said, "I put the bottom stem of the artichoke in the broth or water for more flavor—it is edible and delicious. Cover and bring to a boil for 1/2 to 3/4 of an hour. If need be, moisten the top of each artichoke with water or chicken broth. Test for completeness when a leaf of the artichoke comes out easily."

STILL ALIVE AT 820-822 CHRISTIAN STREET

The Louis E. Ingenito Funeral Home has seen a lot of bodies whose lives depended on the 9th Street Market. Established in 1909, the Ingenitos have embalmed flu victims and various kinds of mobsters and non-mobsters alike. Pat

WOMAN HITS MOUNTED POLICEMAN WITH ROPE IN CHURCH ROW

The scene at the church on Christian Street.
(*Bulletin* photo)

Ingenito likes to say, "I buried 'em all." Located at 822 Christian Street, the funeral home saw the liveliest mob in May of 1933 when its next-door neighbor, Our Lady of Good Counsel Church was closed by Cardinal Dennis Dougherty. Scandals dominated this thirty-five year old parish but His Eminence said that three Catholic Churches within three blocks in the neighborhood was one too much. "Unnecessary?!" A mob quickly gathered on the day the church's doors were to be sealed. Police then arrived in cars or on horseback to subdue the belligerent mob. Bells were rung in protest. Neighbors collected other items to bang and make noise—it was a sign of their anger at their church's closing.

The pizzelle iron was referenced by local newspapers as one of the sources of the clamor. Here's a better use for the iron:

PIZZELLES

6	eggs	1 1/2 C sugar	
3 1/2 C flour		1 T	anise seed
1 T	vanilla extract		

Beat all ingredients together until consistent.

Now, follow the baking directions in the pizzelle iron booklet.

Pizzelle irons may vary in heating.

WAS AT 824 CHRISTIAN STREET

Dr. Anthony LoBianco has the prescription for a sweeter disposition at hand. He came from "Baking Families" with his mother's parents' bakery at 828 Christian Street, "The Martino's", then his parents' shop at 824 Christian which serviced the nine restaurants on 8th Street between Fitzwater and Christian in addition to "Palumbo's." They were busy bakers indeed. In fact, sometimes Mr. LoBianco would ask his son to break away from his medical studies to decorate some cakes, the doctor-to-be's specialty. "I used to bake as a hobby," said the physician who preferred a family practice in his own neighborhood more than the sweetness of his family's profession for about seventy years in Philadelphia.

The LoBianco family was from Agrigento, Sicily while the Martinos were from Messina, a rich Sicilian heritage in creativity with sugar. Likewise, when Dr. LoBianco was asked for a recipe, he arrived at the traditional "Italian Cream Recipe," which his family used in their rum cakes and cannoli. It is presented here in its pure form, in an alternate form and in another way to satisfy our choco-holics—this is one condition which the good doctor probably will not cure!

DR. LoBIANCO'S ITALIAN CREAM FILLING
(Vanilla)

2 qts. whole milk

1 qt. water

Bring these to a boil, but be careful that no burning or scalding occurs.

In separate bowl, mix together:

6 C	sugar	4 C	flour
5	egg yolks	½ C	vanilla extract

"Add 'dry' ingredients slowly to milk-water pot and stir over medium to high heat until boiling begins. Remove from heat, keep stirring and let cool gradually."

For a richer, thicker filling:
   "Add 1 lb. ricotta."

For chocolate-lovers:
   Add 3 C unsweetened cocoa and stir to consistency.

Note: This is a recipe that can fill at least one dozen cannoli and a few cakes. Divide measurements for smaller portions.

840 CHRISTIAN STREET

Want to look "important" on 9th Street?

Wear an apron.

A long one that goes around the neck and covers the thighs.

So positive is the "fashion statement" here of manly men wearing aprons that boys can't wait to put one on and "belong."

Every time one passes "Willie's Water Ice," you'll see the boys wearing starched white aprons and "hangin'" around the window just to "show off" in their aprons. The precedent for this may go back to the 1920s when loitering gangsters often wore aprons atop their expensive tailored suits: it was to suggest to the police that they were indeed working and not to be arrested with the charge as "Suspicious Characters." Joe, the owner at "Willie's Water Ice" makes *fresh* water ice with no preservatives. He does the "hard work" while watching television. You too, can make fresh water ice at home with this recipe.

LEMON WATER ICE

(To make 48 ozs.)

4 C	water	2 C sugar	
2 C	lemon juice	one lemon rind, grated	

Boil water and sugar in saucepan, stirring constantly until a syrup forms. Turn down heat and let cool. Add lemon juice and grated rind. In a blender, add two trays of ice cubes and pour in half of the syrup. One can also adjust the amount of lemon flavor by decreasing the amount of ice for a more lemony taste, or the opposite for a less lemon taste. Blend ice and syrup together so that syrup is evenly distributed.

The next-most popular flavor is, of course...

CHERRY WATER ICE

(for 48 ozs., too)

4 C	water		2 C	sugar
2 C	pureéd maraschino cherries (keep juice in jar)		4 T	lemon juice

Follow directions as above.

842 CHRISTIAN STREET

Dominic "Dukie" Capocci of "Willie's Sandwiches" has a special fan from Washington State who visits him occasionally. The fan is Jeff Smith, "The Frugal Gourmet" who gave Dukie the distinction as the only 9th Street Market area businessman who is in *two* of Smith's cookbooks.

Dukie's "menu" since the early 1930s is just four types of sandwiches: tripe, veal, pork and roast beef. Meatballs in gravy are on weekends. "The Frugal Gourmet" would eat all four sandwiches in one sitting (or standing, if you will) and try to figure how Dukie makes each.

Dukie's Uncle Dan taught him what to do and now Dukie will share his tripe recipe which can be used with macaroni, in an Italian roll or alone in a dish.

WILLIE'S TRIPE

2 lbs. tripe, cut into 1-2" pieces, cleaned and washed

1 T	oil		1	bay leaf
2 T	oregano			salt and pepper
1	(16 oz.) can tomato pureé		2 C	diced onions
1-2 C	diced celery			

Duke said to "get lots of onions and celery and place in pot with oil, bay leaf and oregano. Salt and pepper to taste. Sauté until soft, but not brown. Meanwhile, have the tripe cleaned and washed. Add tripe and about 2 C water to pot and boil until the tripe is half cooked through. Drain water from mixture and add tomato pureé and a little more water. Bring all to a boil and simmer for about one-half hour." Add more water if necessary for a "medium consistency." Tripe should absorb the tomato and create a new taste.

Usually hanging with the guys at 9th and Christian Streets

The "Hinks" man is Charlie "Hinks," a regular guy and frequent sight on 9th Street for "only since about 1927" when his parents brought him there. At age 12, he sold shopping bags at the Market for 3¢. Then after school and on weekends, "seven days a week," he sold produce for Tony Anastasio and got $7.00 as his salary.

Charlie hustled routinely right through high school. The 9th Street Market set his regimen until Uncle Sam drafted him. " 'had to go to war." Charlie's patriotism prevailed through the new routine. Oh, how he missed the weekly food regimen that just about everyone of Italian or Sicilian ancestry in South Philadelphia was accustomed to: "On Sunday it was macaroni; Monday, soup; Tuesday, macaroni again; Wednesday, I forgot; Thursday, macaroni again, Friday, somethin' with fish; then Saturday, I forgot that too." (His wife, Mary will remind him when he eats.)

Returning home from the war, Charlie got his macaroni made by his father, Carlo, the chef at The Brown Derby Restaurant. Then, it was back at the "three times a week macaroni" thing.

But, good Italian cooks know that such meals do not have to be so monotonous. Here, 9th Streeters offer suggestions on what to add to the gravy before you spoon it on the macaroni:

1) "Scungilli. I love it," said Mario Girardo.

2) "Tuna." (Of course!) From Anthony "Lulu" Lucchesi.

3) Pip DeLuca coats a frying pan with a little cooking oil and then throws in leftover macaroni to fry. Different!

4) Coat a baking dish with some oil, add your leftover macaroni (with the gravy already on it) and spread it evenly. Sprinkle generously with cheese (parmesan or romano; we recommend mozzarella) and bake for about 10 minutes at 350°F.

5) stir in some vegetables, such as peas.

6) stir in cooked ground meat.

7) omit any tomato gravy—toss in some butter to the cooked and drained macaroni, add any cheese, parsley (or better, basil) and serve.

WAS AT 901 CHRISTIAN STREET

On the surface, it seems as if it's a man's world on 9th Street: men unloading trucks, men carrying large animal carcasses on their shoulders, men at the produce stands in the worst of weather. But the women are there, some as supportive help, others managing.

Some, like Mr. and Mrs. Frank Giunta like to consider their business as a "100-100" arrangement. Both came from butcher store families around 9th and Christian Streets. They met while young.

They have been inseparable since they met. They do everything together. They almost finish each's sentences. Their eyes talk when they look at each other because they know what the other is thinking. "Yes, everything together," giggled Mrs. Giunta. She laughed because she didn't realize how obvious it is.

Mr. Giunta wanted future admirers of 9th Street to know that once there were seven (7) Giunta butchers at the Market between Christian and Carpenter Streets. His grandfather, Francesco (Frank) was a butcher in 1904 at Delhi and Fitzwater, before 9th Street was a marketplace. The present Frank closed his store with Mrs. Giunta in 1996. Now they're home doing housework and other things—*together.*

Mr. Giunta called with one of Mrs. Giunta's recipes which both enjoy (again the "t" word!)

MRS. GIUNTA'S SAUSAGE, PEPPERS & MUSHROOMS

2 lbs. Italian pork sausage	1	small onion, diced
1 can (16 oz.) tomato puree	1 C	fresh mushrooms
2 C red or green bell peppers, diced	1 bay leaf	

Mr. Giunta said to buy the sausage like he used to make, "with the fennel seed. Brown it first as one piece, then cut it into bitesize pieces. Sauté onion in oil until golden. Add tomato purée, bay leaf and stir on medium heat. Add some water if too thick. Lastly, add peppers to cook with sausages on same temperature. Toss mushrooms in at end and then lower heat." Keep a big loaf of Italian bread nearby to soak up the flavors in the tomato purée.

903-05 CHRISTIAN STREET

Ellis and Sid Shor are Italian by association. As owners of Superior Pasta, they ensure that only the best ingredients are used, such as Granese Cheese, a locally-made Italian cheese that is the only cheese sold in the region that uses its own curd.

Cooking the ready-to-eat meals that are sold there is Clara Quattrone, an employee for about seventeen years who makes "all the sauces, gravies and salads." When Clara was hired to make the manicotti, those large hand-rolled tubes that are filled with ricotta or meat, Clara had no idea that her creations would be on numerous food shows, including Mary Ann Esposito's "Ciao Italia!"

Here's a good one by Clara:

CLARA QUATTRONE'S STEAK PIZZAIUOLO

2 lbs. steak or "frying steak", sliced 1/4" to 1/2" thick

6 oz.	can tomato paste		pinch of meat tenderizer
1/2 C	grated romano	2	cloves garlic, chopped
1/2 C	olive oil	1 t	salt (opt.)
1 t	oregano	1/2 t	black pepper

"Over medium heat, fry steak with olive oil for about 20 to 30 minutes with other ingredients, except the cheese. Add some water, 1/2 C at a time if the oil evaporates during the cooking. When the water is absorbed, add tomato paste with one can of water that rinsed residue from can. Add more water if necessary. Let everything cook together. Lastly, add the cheese and let it simmer into the meat for a few minutes."

Clara recommends serving a large Italian salad on the side of this entrée that feeds about four.

WAS AT 910 CHRISTIAN STREET

Born in 1914, Joseph Litto, Sr.'s life was always sweet.

His grandfather, Giovanni Tropea had a pushcart on 9th Street but his father, Orazio said, "Let's stay with the cakes!" because it was better than hawking produce. His mother played a part in the baking of the cakes as well by reading the marriage licenses listed in the newspapers and contacting the espoused. She then showed them photos of Litto's wedding cakes and the sales were consummated.

But that was the cake situation before the war!

When Joe got drafted, "The bakery saved my life [because] I was a baker for Eisenhower's headquarters in Kingston, England." His rank was Bakery Sergeant. (Honest!) "I must have been a good Bakery Sergeant—a dessert every day—because someone took my name off the list to go to the fronts." About two weeks after the war's over, the Army took Joe to Germany to set up a bakery at the U.S. barracks there. It didn't last too long: a fungus on his hands forced Sergeant Litto to open a "club" for the enlisted men. "I made the D.P.'s (displaced persons) waiters." Eventually, Sgt. Litto had to come back home and resume baking cakes, this time for the G.I.s and post-war brides. He and his family would cater weddings with a buffet "for $1,600.00 and for 150 to 200 people including the wedding cake!"

Litto's Bakery was resurrected in the 1990s, but closed in January, 1998. "I loved 9th Street." Those were sweet memories for Joe.

Mr. Litto has some baking tips:

1) use butter-flavored vegetable shortening instead of butter in cakes. "Butter makes cakes too tender...they fall apart."

2) "There's nothing like a fresh egg coming from the shell." Try not to use the powdered stuff. "Especially for sponge cakes, use real eggs."

3) There's no substitute for real sugar. Sorry!

4) use semi-sweet chocolate and regulate the amount of sugar to make it sweeter.

5) "If you only have one type of flour to use, sift it for a more refined flour for pastry and cakes. Breads use a harder flour."

6) Flavorings: "Nutmeg, vanilla and butter flavors for my poundcakes. Vanilla, just vanilla for sponge. And rum flavoring, not real rum, for rum cakes."

"EVERYBODY'S BUDDY!"

The consummate politician, former State Senator Henry "Buddy" Cianfrani began negotiating with food ingredients "about 15 years ago. I like to fool around in the kitchen. I'm good at pastas, gravies, marinara sauce, pasta 'n cec'— I make it for the club." It is a great satisfaction for him to cook. Buddy is particular in what ingredients he uses and said emphatically that "Fiorella's sausage" is the only sausage that he will buy and eat.

For the 9th Street Italian Market, Buddy was and still is there to help: "I was with them with the construction of 9th Street with the money. Whatever their needs were, I was there." Service to the Market goes back further to the 1960s when the then-movable pushcarts crowded the street. Buddy guaranteed all that an unlimited number of carts could be on the street. "I made a grandfather clause—whoever had a cart [already] on 9th Street could stay where they were."

That's why he's our buddy, Buddy!

BUDDY CIANFRANI'S HOME-MADE CUP CUSTARD

3	eggs	3 C	milk
3/4 C	sugar	1 oz.	brandy
cinnamon		nutmeg	

"In a large bowl, blend the eggs, milk, sugar and brandy to consistency. Place this mixture in a container that is surrounded with water. Sprinkle with cinnamon and nutmeg on top."

Preheat oven at 350°F on bake—"Cook 1 hour 10 minutes. Remove from the oven and let it cool. Then place in the fridge till ready to serve. If you prefer you can add raisins to mixture before cooking."

WAS AT 904 CHRISTIAN STREET

That Millie Testa Vanni is so full of love!

When neighbors pass by her, they stroke her cheek.

Or they greet her with a combination of affection in the tilt of the head in the "Hi, Millie!" and an impulse to touch the gracious lady whose blue eyes dance in warmth. Millie just takes in all of the attention because after all, that's what the

Now a parking lot, Christian Street at Darien c. 1900 used to provide various services for immigrants and transatlantic travellers. To the far right is Luigi Fiorella's "Meat Market," one of the first butcher stores in "Little Italy" and now entering its third century here.

youngest children in families do best. Millie is the proud recipient of love from her older seven Testa siblings, their children and their children's children.

The Testa family had a mutual fondness for the Italian Market. Salvatore Testa, Millie's much revered father, began his chicken store at 904 Christian Street just before 1920. "He was called Salvatore, Tore and Sam but no one could call him 'chicken,'" mused Millie. The family's strength however, came from the love Salvatore had for wife, Maria which then extended to their eight children. Love is all that Millie knows. So it's natural for her to describe the 9th Street Market of her youth: "Lots of love, energy, very hard work and so much fun went into those times. When I look back through tears of nostalgia, I feel such love!"

The family's store closed in the 1960s but memories live on, such as in these family recipes that Millie shares, along with her love.

ROASTED CHICKEN a la FAMIGLIA TESTA

6-7 lb. roasting chicken, with skin on.		1/2 C	olive oil
2-3	large white potatoes	1	peeled lemon or orange
2-3	large sweet potatoes	2	onions, sliced into quarters

salt, black pepper, Italian seasoning and garlic powder
use from 1 T or more of each, depending on size of chicken

"Wash and dry chicken, removing insides. Place chicken in roasting pan after sprinkling the entire bird with seasonings. Stuff the cavity of the chicken with the lemon (or orange.) Pour olive oil and 1 C of water over the chicken. Cover chicken in pan and back for one hour at 350°F. Then, uncover chicken and let bake for an additional 1 1/4 hours. After baking, drain liquid and arrange chicken and potatoes on serving dish." Serves 6 to 8.

CONNIE TESTA'S DELICIOUS CHICKEN

3-4 lbs. chicken wings and legs		1 C	olive oil
2 C	bread crumbs (Italian seasoned)		

"Wash and dry chicken, leaving skin on. Dip chicken in olive oil, then coat in bread crumbs. Lay on cookie sheet and cover with aluminum foil and bake for one hour at 350°F. Uncover, then bake an additional hour or until golden brown." Millie said that her dear sister never turned the pieces over while cooking. "It's a delicious treat. Enjoy!" said Millie.

ST. PAUL'S CHURCH: 923 CHRISTIAN STREET

Frances Giunta Giordano was a religious woman in her own way. She was very generous to St. Paul's Church which explains why the "Paul and Frances Giordano" name is frequently seen in the church.

St. Paul's religious dine well too, courtesy of the ladies who, like Mrs. Giordano, want to make sure that the clergy are comfortable.

Julia Polito Lauria grew up on 9th Street where her father had a stand. "He was the only one who washed his greens on the stand every day." Now, Julia still lives and shops at 9th Street while as a secretary to the priests at St. Paul's. Julia shares cooking duties with Sandy, another neighborhood lady, who do their work religiously. Their cooking makes parishioners invoke the Lord. Go to Mass at St. Paul's at 5 P.M. on Saturdays or 11 A.M. on Sundays and you'll say, "My God! What smells so good?" It's the aromas coming from the rectory kitchen.

The church ladies have donated these recipes which they use to cook for St. Paul's "men of God."

SANDY AMOROSO'S NAPOLITANO PIE
(An Easter Treat)

8 to 10 eggs, beaten	3 lbs.	ricotta
1½ C sugar	½ C	pignoli nuts
1 t vanilla extract	¼ C	baby pastina (before cooking)
		salt to cook pastina

"Cook pastina as directed, drain and put aside. Preheat oven at 350°F. Grease and flour 9" spring form or Bundt-type pan. Mix all ingredients with cooked pastina and pour into pan and bake for 1¼ to 2 hours or until done."

Makes a pie that will serve ten or more.

JULIA POLITO LAURIA'S STUFFED PEPPERS
(Vegetarian-Style)

6	bell peppers, cored	½ loaf fresh American bread or
2	eggs	5	Kaiser or Italian rolls
¾ C	locatelli cheese	3	cloves mashed garlic
¼ C	fresh parsley	1 can (8 oz.) tomato sauce

"Stuff raw peppers with all ingredients except tomato sauce. Place in baking pan and pour tomato sauce over peppers. Cover to bake at 350°F for about 1 hour or until peppers are soft, but not burned."

RESTORES SENSE OF HISTORY IN NEIGHBORHOOD.

Jim Campenella's view of the Italian Market neighborhood is usually from deep under the foundations of the buildings where he has found the bones and stones of another time. He has maintained St. Paul's Church's 1843 dignity with his restoration work in the wooden carvings, marble, walls and stained glass. His construction company developed buildings atop the old "Cuneo and Lagomarsino

Maccaroni Factory" at Eighth and Christian Streets and where some of the old cemeteries faced the Baldwin Locomotive lines on Washington Avenue.

"I run the whole operation—residential, commercial, industrial, restoration and new construction," said Jim. His mark is everywhere around the Italian Market. Jim's parents' roots were in the Market neighborhood and he chose it as his home near St. Paul's Church. He watches the Market with an engineer's eye but he also enjoys what the Market sells.

Jim's recipe is inspired by his Neapolitan ancestry.

JIM CAMPENELLA'S MANICOTTI WITH CHEESE FILLING

Manicotti:

6 eggs, at room temperature	1 1/2 C unsifted all-purpose flour
1/4 t salt	

Filling:

2 lbs. ricotta cheese	1/3 C parmesan cheese, grated
1 pkg. (8 oz.) mozzarella, diced	2 eggs
1/4 t pepper	1 t salt
1/4 C parmesan cheese, grated (to be used after cooking)	1 T parsley, chopped

"In a medium bowl, combine the eggs, flour and salt and 1 1/2 C water. With an electric mixer, beat until smooth. Let stand 1/2 hour or longer. Slowly heat an 8" non-stick skillet. Pour in 3 T batter, rotating the skillet quickly to spread the batter evenly over the bottom. Cook over medium heat until the top is dry but the bottom is not brown. Turn out on a wire rack to cool. Continue until all of the batter is used. As the manicotti cool, stack them with waxed paper between them. Preheat oven to 350°F.

"In a large bowl, combine ricotta, mozzarella, 1/3 C parmesan, eggs, salt, pepper and parsley. Spread about 1/4 C filling down the center of each manicotti and roll them up. Spoon 1 1/2 C sauce into each of two 12x8x2" baking dishes. Place eight rolled manicotti seam side down, in single layers; top with five more. Cover with 1 C sauce, sprinkle with more parmesan. Bake uncovered 1/2 hour or until bubbly."

WAS AT 11TH & CHRISTIAN STREETS

Local "wiseguys" (a/k/a, Mafiosi) ate well in the neighborhood restaurants that purchased most of their food from the 9th Street Market. Many "Last Suppers" of the gangsters came directly from 9th Street too, whether from an eaterie or their mothers' home cooking.

The neighborhood "guys" knew good food from bad, but no restaurant had an association with the guys more than the former "Cous' Little Italy," also known as "Torano's" at 11th and Christian Streets. A succession of "allegeds" and "reputeds" owned this bar/restaurant for almost fifty years. But there was also a following from the general public who loved the restaurant's fine food. Philadelphia's former mob boss, Angelo Bruno ate Torano's Chicken Sicilian before he was driven to his death.

Former chef/owner of Torano's, Robert Barretta offers a version of this dish which also reflects his training in New York's "Little Italy."

CHICKEN SICILIAN di ROBERT BARRETTA

4 (8 oz. each) boneless & skinless chicken breasts, cut into 1" cubes and
    lightly floured
1 whole Spanish onion, sliced
3 T   each blended oil and a good olive oil
8   cloves garlic, sliced into slithers
16   whole cherry peppers, de-stemmed and de-seeded
1/2 C imported Gaeta olives or Greek or oil-cured Sicilian olives (must be pitted)
1 T   fresh oregano, basil and parsley (each)

1/2 t	coarse black pepper	1/2 t	kosher salt
1C	white wine	1	stick butter
1 T	capers	2 C	chicken stock

"In a large pan, sauté on medium heat the chicken in *blended oil* until brown on all sides. Strain the oil from the pan and add the 3 tbs. olive oil, garlic, onion and sauté for 1 to 3 minutes. When onions are translucent, add the white wine and cherry peppers, olives and capers. Simmer for 1 to 3 minutes. Add chicken stock and simmer for 3 to 5 minutes to reduce stock. Roll the stick of butter in flour and add to the pan with the mix. Then, add the fresh herbs last and simmer for another 3 to 5 minutes. Sauce will gradually thicken. Serve immediately."

Serves four.

902 1/2 SOUTH 9TH STREET

Our Millie Testa's nostalgic memories of the 9th Street culture included some sandwich-makers that typified the times, such as the man who sold "Juice Sandwiches," and for those with a few pennies more, the men who sold sandwiches with meats. Olga Vellios' father, George, who was from Greece, had a stand at 9th and Christian Streets selling hot dogs, hamburgers and their famous "barbecue." Just what is the "barbecue"? Olga said that it was her mother's concoction: "She knew what to do with the 9th Street butchers' meat scraps—add hot peppers, vinegar, red cherry peppers...that's what they used then."

The "barbecue" recipe has changed over the years to suit customers' tastes. But, we really don't want Olga to divulge what is in their best seller at the sandwich shop. So, Olga gives us her friend Millie's favorite, "Pita," which is a shorter, easier way to say, "Greek Spinach Pie!"

THE VELLIOS FAMILY'S SPINACH PIE

3 lbs.	fresh chopped spinach	3	"bunches" scallions
3	leeks (or "one bunch")	3	eggs, beaten
1/2 lb.	feta cheese	3-4 T	flour
2 T	parsley	1	stick butter or margarine
1/4 C	or more olive oil	1 lb.	(15 to 20 sheets) philo

"In a large, deep pot, mix spinach, scallions, leeks, cheese and parsley. Spinach is very watery and should be drained before laying it onto the dough," said Olga.

"Grease an 18"x18" pan and line it with about 5 sheets of dough that was brushed with the oil/butter mix. Leave any excess dough hanging over pan. Spread about 1/2 spinach mix over dough. Take another 5 sheets of dough that was brushed on both sides with the oil/butter mix and lay on top of spinach. Spread remaining spinach mix atop dough and repeat with another 5 sheets of brushed dough on this last layer. Bake in oven at 350°F for about 20 minutes. Dough will turn golden and flakey on bottom," so Olga suggested to "turn pie upside down for same golden, flakey texture. The sides should be turned towards the top so as to fold the dough into an "envelope" for the spinach filling."

This is a large pie that can feed about ten adults or more (or less if they really like it!)

SPICE GIRLS WITH STAYING POWER

The South 9th Street Market has its own Spice Girls, Marie and Annette who know more about real spices than anyone. Just ask any question and they have the answers on herbs, spices, rices, coffees, teas and flavorings that are their lives and livelihoods at the Market.

Annette LaTerza submitted this recipe by her parents that is a "downtown" favorite.

JOHN & MARIE LaTERZA'S "JUMBOT"

5	medium potatoes	2	large eggplants
2 (each)	red, green and yellow peppers, sliced	3 t	dried basil
1	medium onion, chopped	2 T	olive oil
5	cloves, garlic, minced	3	tomatoes, chopped
1 lb.	mushrooms, sliced		salt & pepper to taste

"Peel potatoes and eggplant. Dice and set them aside. In a large dutch oven, sauté in the olive oil the garlic and onion until they are soft. Use a low to medium heat. Add peppers and cook until peppers are halfway done. Then add the eggplant, mushrooms and chopped tomatoes, salt, pepper and basil.

"Cook with the lid on, letting the steam out for about one hour or until the potatoes are soft."

Serve with some crusty Italian bread.

WAS AT 910 SOUTH 9TH STREET

"Cat calls" are not the only sounds on 9th Street but they may be the only "animal" sounds left from a marketplace that used to sell live animals, such as baby goats and lambs in cages on the street. So cute to kids. So delicious to adults. Carmen Lerro remembered when he had to go to the slaughterhouse up the street: "The lamb sounded like 'ma-ah, ma-ma-ah' like it was calling for its mother" before it became mutton. Dominic Venuto, born at 900 South 9th Street and living later at 910 and other places on the Market recalled, "We were like checkers on the street" moving around. He had the largest veal and lamb business in Philadelphia once. Now he claims to have had the last slaughterhouse in the city. It closed in 1996.

Venuto's fresh meats were sold on 9th Street for about sixty years. "My roots, my heritage is on 9th Street," he emotes. Dominic Venuto said that he used a more humane way for us to eat the steak sandwiches, veal cutlets and Jell-O on which most of us grew up.

Dominic and his sister, Jean Venuto Franklin decided to lend this recipe which always makes Dominic's mouth water.

THE VENUTO FAMILY'S BEEF "BRACCIOLTINES"

2 lbs. top of the round beef sliced thin ("fina, fina") or bracciole steak sheets

1 C	bread crumbs	2	cloves garlic, mashed
1/4 C	fresh parsley	1 C	olive oil in flat dish
1/2 C	grated parmesan cheese	salt & pepper to taste	

Anthony Bonuomo in his butcher store, 910 South 9th Street. c. 1950.

(Photo courtesy, Agnes Bonuomo Viso)

"In a bowl, mix bread crumbs, parsley, cheese and garlic. You might just want to add a pinch of pepper if the cheese is salted. Dip each piece of steak into oil, on both sides. Lay steak sheet open and add some of the mix. Roll each up and either use skewers or tie the small bundles with some string to prevent from opening.

"Place in a broiler pan at 400°F for 10 to 15 minutes, then turn over and broil for 10-15 minutes. Add to gravy, if preferred."

Was at 910 South 9th Street (After Venuto)

Oh! What's that? This store is the closest to a "museum" at the Italian Market. Walking past 910 South 9th Street, one is attracted to what seems like a butcher store from the 1920s. Antonio, or just "Tony" Bonuomo from Foggia, Italy, whom 9th Streeters regarded with respect and affection, ran his store for just over fifty years here. "He just had so many qualities," said his daughter, Agnes Bonuomo Viso. Tony sold meats here that were freshly slaughtered at his abatoir. "At that time, people bought 'halves' in butcher stores," said Tony's son-in-law, Buddy Viso. A "steel" was used to sharpen knives; a cleaver; a hand saw; a steak knife and a boning knife—all a butcher needed in his trade.

Tony passed away in 1979, remembered for his generosity and kindness. Today, only Tony's butcher store remains as his legacy for those who missed the sight of his smile.

Agnes Viso gives these recipes:

SWEETBREADS a la AGGIE

2 lbs. sweetbreads	olive oil on side	
2 T	garlic powder	1/4 C or more parmesan cheese
3-4	fresh tomatoes, sliced	salt & pepper to taste
2-3 T fresh parsley	2 T	oregano

"Rinse sweetbreads and then boil them in salted water for about 15 minutes. When cooled, peel the membranes off. Slice the sweetbreads in half and place in oiled baking dish. Then sprinkle with salt, pepper, oregano, parsley, cheese and lay slices of the tomatoe on top. Bake in oven at 350°F for about 25 minutes."

SWEETBREADS a la AGGIE #2

2 lbs. sweetbreads	3	eggs, beaten
1/3 C grated parmesan cheese	2 C	Italian seasoned bread crumbs
3-4 C blended oil to fry		

"Rinse and boil sweetbreads as indicated above to remove the membranes. When membranes are removed, dip each sweetbread into egg and cheese mix, then into the bread crumbs and fry in skillet until done."

WAS AT 911 SOUTH 9TH STREET

Want to say, "Ah!" again? "D'Orazio's!"

Anthony D'Orazio, now in Bellmawr, New Jersey waxed about how his great-uncle, Antonio Giannone came from Sicily and decided to settle down at 911 South 9th Street and make ricotta.

"Ah…"

This simple Sicilian's legacy to his grand-nephews caused their business to expand three times since they left the 9th Street Italian Market. Now one has to go to the local supermarket to buy D'Orazio ravioli, manicotti or other fine products.

Theresa Giannone D'Orazio was 92 years young before leaving us. She retired from the Italian cheese business at age 78 after living her life and raising a family on 9th Street near Christian. Her son, Anthony credited his life experience on 9th Street as a lesson in the work ethic. Of course, they miss the Market of the past! But they still cook and bake as on 9th Street, as with Mrs. D'Orazio's "Two-Tone Ricotta Pie!"

MRS. D'ORAZIO'S TWO-TONE RICOTTA CHEESE PIE

Cream Filling:

1 qt. milk		8	egg yolks
1 C sugar		1/2 C	corn starch (to add to milk)
grated peel of one lemon		2-3	cinnamon sticks

Cheese Filling:

1 1/2 lbs.ricotta		6	eggs
1 C sugar			

In bowl:

Cream 6 eggs and sugar together, then fold in ricotta. Set aside.

In 2-3 quart saucepan:

"Over medium heat, cook milk, eggs, sugar and corn starch. Stir for consistency and keep stirring over heat to prevent from sticking on bottom of pan. Lastly, add lemon peel and cinnamon sticks. When filling thickens, remove sticks.

"Line a Bundt-type of pan that is at least three inches deep with a graham cracker or other soft cookie crust on bottom and sides. Spoon ricotta filling on bottom evenly, then spoon atop this the *cooled* cream/cinnamon filling. Sprinkle with any leftover crust crumbs. Bake at 325° F for one hour. Serve when cooled."

THE MARKET'S FUTURE:
AT 911 AND 913 SOUTH 9TH STREET

Tran and Nguyen Ho would probably be woking rather than working on 9th Street if they had their way. Everyone likes this jovial couple who sell outerware and some small electronics at the Market which is becoming less Italian and more Asian. They are an example of the wonderful people in the ethnic evolution of the neighborhood.

Tran and Nguyen are Chinese and obviously cook together as they gave me this recipe together. (Are they related to the Giuntas?) Together, they decided that this is the best dish for Americans to try to wok at.

SIMPLY DELICIOUS CHICKEN FRIED RICE

In a wok, coat with vegetable oil. Tran prefers this brand of oil rather than others.

Add to oiled and heated wok:

1	small onion, diced	1/2 C	beansprouts (add last)
1/2 C	scallions, diced	1 lb.	chicken breast, diced

In saucepan:

"Boil water and add 1 C rice until water evaporates while cooking. Add rice to heated wok and stir with 1 teaspoon soy sauce ("for color") and a little salt.

"Throw in beansprouts last on top of chicken/rice mix." Serves four.

Tran and Nguyen say this dish is this easy to do.

Scott and Judy Tran, meanwhile, offer a challenging Asian dish:

WONDERFUL STIR FRY

1/2 lb.	snow peas	1/2 can	bamboo shoots
1/2 can	baby corn	1 can	mushrooms
1 t	sesame oil	2 t	oyster sauce
1/2 lb.	rump of pork, diced	1/2 lb.	shrimp
1/2 lb.	scallops	3 T	corn oil
1 t	sugar	3-4	cloves garlic (mashed)
1 t	soy sauce	1/2 t	salt
1 t	cornstarch in 1/4 C water to make a paste	salt to taste	

"In the wok, put oil, garlic, pork, mushrooms, babycorn and fry. Add seafood and rest of ingredients. Lastly, add soy sauce and mix into stir fry. Remove food from wok immediately."

Judy suggested to "marinate pork with oyster sauce for a few hours before woking." For the adventurous, Judy added 1/2 t MSG to meat.

91

WAS AT 918 SOUTH 9TH STREET

The Michael Maggio Cheese Company began as a humble grocery store at 918 South 9th Street in the 1920s. Like many businesses, Maggio's began to specialize in the cheeses they made on the street while their general line of grocery merchandize gradually phased out. With Mr. Maggio, bigger was indeed better and his cheesemaking expanded into a factory at the Market.

Imagine a ricotta and mozzarella factory on 9th Street, emitting those mouth-watering aromas to anyone alive and breathing on the street! (The factory was just about 50 feet from The Italian Burial Casket Company!)

The M. Maggio Cheese Company went on to become what may be reported as the largest Italian cheese producer in Pennsylvania. In 1998, the family-owned business was sold, but the name lives on with the new owners because of its fine reputation in its products.

This cheese recipe is versatile and can be used to fill large macaroni shells, ravioli, lasagna, eggplant rolls, zucchini, fish or meats. It will also make you smile when you say, "Cheese!"

CHEESE FILLING

2 lbs.	ricotta	2	eggs
1/2 lb.	shredded mozzarella	1/2 C	any "grating" cheese
1 T	onion salt	2 T	parsley (or more)
salt and pepper to taste			

Mix all of the ingredients together and then use according to your recipe for the macaroni, etc.

WAS AT 920 SOUTH 9TH STREET

Parents get blamed for the darnest reasons.

Frankie DiPietro, born in 1920, blames his beloved mother on introducing him to the 9th Street Market at age 13. One day, Mrs. DiPietro brought her young son to 9th Street and asked Mr. Attilio Esposito, "Would you teach my son?" Frankie cleaned the butcher store and did odd jobs for a year before leaving Esposito's for Cappuccio's Meat where he spent the next seventeen years. Then he started his own retail meat business, named after himself, "Frankie's."

Two men from the Chicago Meat Board came to the 9th Street Market recently and found that only Frankie sold fresh hanging beef. The significance?

"Everyone uses boxed, dry-o-vac meat that may have been left two weeks or longer in the freezer." The meat inspector is at the slaughterhouse before or just after the animal is put down. A grader then judges the meat to be either "prime," "choice" or "good." "Select" or "ungraded" meat are the lowest levels. Anthony, Frankie's son, said that his father can look at an animal and "tell if it will taste good." Their meats have a money-back guarantee. Honest!

Eleanor DiPietro DeFrancesco, Frankie's daughter submits this recipe for veal medallions, a popular sale item at the store.

THE DiPIETRO FAMILY'S VEAL MEDALLIONS

1 T	olive oil	1 T	butter
2-3 T	basil	salt and pepper to taste	
1 lb.	veal scallops		

Sauté veal in oil and butter. "When it turns white, it's done." Add remaining ingredients and stir. Serve it atop spaghetti. You can add white wine in the pan while the veal is cooking and then drink the wine with the meal afterward.

Serves four with 1 lb. of spaghetti.

DIED AT 924-926 SOUTH 9TH STREET

Of the many ironies in and around the 9th Street Market, it is difficult to believe that a place bursting with the elements of life and joyful living would also remind shoppers of death.

From the 1920s to about the mid-1940s, pushcart vendors and street hucksters made room for the arrivals of corpses and the exits of coffins from The Italian Burial Casket Company at 9th and Hall Streets. Founded by Pietro Jacovini, one of the neighborhood's most enterprising businessmen, the company arranged for the burials of many on and off 9th Street.

Alfonso Baldi came to Philadelphia in 1902 and started his own funeral business on the corner of 9th and Wharton Streets. The flu of 1918 raging Philadelphia apparently gave him a solid financial base to leave his brother, C.C.A.'s firm and to establish his own.

By the 1940s, the Baldi and Jacovini funeral businesses were off 9th Street, away from the Market and on Broad Street where they still survive today, alive and well.

"Consolation Soup" was usually made for mourners after a funeral. Some people in South Philadelphia also call it "Wedding Soup" or just plain "'scadole soup." Here, we call it...

JOAN DiLODOVICO BALDI'S ESCAROLE SOUP

"In an 8-10 quart pot, over boiling water place:

1 (about 5 lbs. or more) whole chicken with insides removed

4 to 5	carrots, diced	4-5	celery stalks, diced, include leaves as well
2	bay leaves		

salt & pepper to taste

"Boil all ingredients together until chicken is done. Skim off any fat residue on top. Set aside.

"In another large pot, boil until half cooked:

1½ large heads of escarole which has been cut into 1" pieces. Then, in frying pan sauté 3 diced cloves of garlic in about 2 tablespoons of olive oil.

Do not burn. Add some water to escarole and simmer.

"Meatball ingredients:

1½ lb.	ground veal	½ C	bread crumbs
1	clove minced garlic	⅓ C	locatelli cheese
1	egg	2 T	chopped Italian parsley

salt & pepper to taste

"Mix ingredients together, then make small meatballs." Joan likes very small, about ½" wide balls. "Add to chicken broth and let simmer. Lastly, add escarole. Flake chicken and add to soup. Stir. This should serve 4 to 6 very hungry adults."

924-926 SOUTH 9TH STREET

The hearty people from the town of Montella have been migrating to Philadelphia for over one hundred years, adding their culinary contributions to the local markets. Montellese Antonio Marano's macaroni, the staple of late 19th century immigrants has given way to the "nouveau cuisine" of late 20th century Montellese cooking, as seen here with Salvatrice Russo Auriemma's recipes.

Mrs. Auriemma's husband was Claudio a man who tug on everyone's heart-strings at the 9th Street Market. Born in Montella, he founded his "Claudio's King of Cheese" store in about 1964 on 9th Street where his sons continue his business.

Otherwise known as "Mrs. Auriemma" or "Sally" (or "Mom" to her handsome children) this beautiful woman's cooking shows an evolution in regional cuisine where more elaborate ingredients make more interesting as well as healthy dishes. Three of Mrs. Auriemma's recipes are given here to illustrate native Montellese cooking at its best.

"MELENZANE MONTELLESA"

2 to 3 large ripe eggplants (or enough for 16 slices)

1 C   all-purpose flour

2   eggs, beaten   salt to keep on side

2 C   olive oil   2 qts. Basic Tomato Sauce

1 lb.   prosciutto, sliced thin   (See recipe that follows)

1 lb.   mozzarella, sliced thin

"Slice eggplants length-wise and very thin, about 1/4" thick. Try to make 16 slices. Then, generously salt both sides of each eggplant slice and lay on a cool rack for about 1 hour. Moisture from the eggplant will bead on the surface. After about 1 hour, blot the surface with a paper towel and brush off excess salt. Pour oil into a large sauté pan to a depth of about 2 inches and place on medium heat. Coat eggplant slices in flour, then dip into beaten eggs. Fry in oil and when cooked, drain on paper towels. Let all 16 slices cool. Place one slice of prosciutto and 1 slice of cheese down atop each other and roll it with each slice of eggplant. Place the 16 slices in a casserole or baking dish.

"Cover rolls with the Basic Tomato Sauce and bake at 375°F for about 10 to 15 minutes or until heated through."

SALLY AURIEMMA'S "BASIC TOMATO SAUCE"

2 qts. canned plum tomatoes ("Using Salvatrice Auriemma's home-jarred plum tomatoes elevates this dish to unparalleled heights.")

6   whole fresh garlic cloves   1 C   fresh basil leaves

salt & pepper to taste

"Combine all above ingredients together and cook over low to medium heat for 1/2 to 1 hour. This can be used on any pasta or dish."

Another "unparalleled" recipe from Mrs. Auriemma. (This one she made for Ristorante Panorama!)

"SPALAGI a la SALVATRICE"

1   bunch of asparagus (roughly one pound)

1/2 lb. prosciutto   2 T   capers

2   cloves of garlic, chopped   2 T   chopped parsley

1/2 C   olive oil   juice of one hole lemon

shredded parmegiano cheese

about 1 C (or more, if preferred) roasted peppers

"Grill the asparagus on the rack in a broiler for about 5 minutes on each side. Wrap the prosciutto around bunches of 6 stalks of asparagus. Place on a dish. In separate bowl, combine the capers, garlic, olive oil, lemon and parsley. Pour this over the bunches of asparagus."

"Top with the shredded parmegiano cheese and roasted peppers."

Serves 2 to 3 individuals as an appetizer.

930 SOUTH 9TH STREET

Pauciello's, D'Orazio's, Mancuso's, Cucinotta's and Maggio's.

They were the cheesemakers and sellers on 9th Street before Danny DiBruno decided that he didn't want to follow in his father's footsteps at the produce stands at 9th and League Streets. Instead, he established "DiBruno's House of Cheese" in 1939 after learning more about cheeses during a trip to Switzerland.

Darling Danny is gone, but his sister, Rita DiBruno Sulpizio gives one of her Abruzzese family recipes that uses cheese.

THE DiBRUNO FAMILY'S "MINIAZ'"

1 lb.	perciatelli, cooked and drained		
6	eggs, beaten with coarse black pepper (to taste)	1/2 C	locatelli cheese
			salt to taste

"Aunt" Rita said, "The coarser the black pepper, the better."

"Mix the cooked and drained macaroni together with the wet eggs. Then place into a greased cooking pan and bake in the oven until the eggs are baked—maybe in about 1/2 hour at 300°F."

When finished cooking, cut the macaroni into square pieces.

"It cooks like a pie, which is great," added "Aunt" Rita of this quick dish.

Danny DiBruno on far right with his brothers and some customers, c. 1940.
(Photo courtesy DiBruno's House of Cheese's Mignucci cousins)

932-36 SOUTH 9TH STREET

Maybe it's because "Roma" spelt backwards is "Amor," Latin for "love," that there's more cooking at this restaurant than spaghetti sometimes.

There's that look that only a Sicilian gives that can scare. Sicilians talk alot with their eyes although the din on 9th Street probably overstates even the unspoken words. Here's the story of two Sicilians with too much pride to speak their minds:

"She said: 'I was walking north on 9th Street and he was walking south when we first saw each other in front of the dumpsters. That's when lightning struck me—it's the only way that I can explain it. We didn't say anything—we just looked at each other." He just stares. "When he first kissed me in the Villa di Roma, I felt as if I was whacked in the head with a sledgehammer. I went unconscious. It was wonderful (the kiss.)"

Don't even try to figure this out!

Pip DeLuca of the Villa di Roma gave the appropriate dish for this story:

PIP DeLUCA'S CHICKEN LIVERS ROMANO

1 pint container of livers will amply serve 2 voracious lovers. Pip said to "lightly fry the livers in a saucepan with about...

    4 T   cooking oil and

    3 medium onions, diced (or 1½ C chopped)

"After the livers and onions are browned, but not thoroughly cooked through, add to the pan:

    1 C   green peppers, chopped and diced

    1 C   mushrooms

    salt and pepper to taste

    ½ t   garlic powder (or more to taste)

then add:

    3 to 4 oz. lightly salted butter

    ¼ C   red "house wine," (or more if you want)

"Simmer livers and other ingredients on low to medium heat until cooked."

This dish can be served alone or over medium cut macaroni or over rice.

97

937 SOUTH 9TH STREET

A lady should never be asked her age but Antoinette Cannuli will tell you that she was born on "January 30, 1910 in Philadelphia." The matriarch of the Cannuli family will also tell you how the "House of Pork" was established shortly after her marriage in 1929. The tall beauty was in an arranged marriage that was typical of the Sicilian middleclass. She was young and worried. When her new husband temporarily lost use of his right arm, his butchering arm, Mrs. Cannuli learned to cut meat as he taught her to do his work, bonding closer. Loving.

Mrs. Cannuli's affection for her workers is evident throughout the store. And the affection is returned. No matter what the ethnicity of the employee, they all call her, "Grandmom." She's the boss at work with her hair pinned in pretty French curls and long white lab coat. You have to love her.

This is Mrs. Cannuli's recipe for rabbit-stew, Sicilian-style.

RABBIT STEW a la GRANDMOM CANNULI

1	whole rabbit, cut into pieces	2 T	oil
1/2	glass red wine	1/2 C	diced onions
2	cloves garlic, diced	1	(8 oz.) can whole tomatoes
3 T	parsley	1 T	garlic salt
1	bay leaf, crushed	1/2 C	chopped celery
black pepper to taste		2-3 C	diced potatoes (opt.)

"Soak rabbit in water and salt overnight. Rinse rabbit the next day and pat dry. Brown rabbit in oiled frying pan, then add onions and garlic and stir." Add red wine and cover, "so the smell stays inside." Keep on medium heat until rabbit is cooked. Add tomatoes and spices, celery and potatoes until potatoes are cooked. "I like to add whole tomatoes in it instead of pureéd tomatoes" which some people use.

Any further instructions? "My house is always open...my heart more."

937 SOUTH 9TH STREET

Charles Cannuli, Jr. loves his pigs and they seem to be everywhere: at the Jersey shore, in numerous bars, at executive parties and at Pat's Steaks. But Charlie does things with his pigs that no one else does. He grew up with the pigs, the third generation to specialize in roasted pigs. Yet, Charlie is never satisfied with an ordinary pork roast. Ask him what you can do with his pigs and you'll get a textbook of recipes, all originals from this amateur chef.

At first, Charlie didn't know which one of his many pork recipes he'd give—they are all different and taste differently. "Alright, try this one," he said of this unbelievably tasty pork dish.

CHARLIE CANNULI'S STUFFED PORK LOIN WRAPPED IN BACON

2	(about 3 lbs. each) boneless center-cut pork loin (make sure both are the same size and length)		
4	garlic cloves, chopped fine	2 T	ground black pepper
2 T	crushed bay leaf		dash of salt
1 1/2 lb.	Italian mild pork sausage (without casing)		
1/2 lb.	slab bacon, sliced thin	1 T	hot pepper
1 C	chicken stock or broth	1 T	rosemary

Serves about 10 people.

"With pork loins open, place sausage in centers and close both loins together with string or butchers' cord. Tie tight so that a bundle is formed. Combine spices together separately and then rub the outside of the loins with the seasonings. Lay strips of bacon atop loin bundle and lay in roasting pan with the chicken stock. Bake in oven at 350°F for 2 1/2 hours or until done."

Grandmom and Grandpop Cannuli at 938 South 9th Street. c. 1950.

(Photo courtesy, Charles Cannuli)

"O.K., Charlie, what do you eat as a side dish for this?"

PORCINI MUSHROOMS

2 lbs. porcini mushrooms, cut into pieces

2   cloves of garlic, diced   1/2 stick butter

salt & pepper to taste

"Sauté garlic in butter and add mushrooms, stirring constantly. Season to taste."

945 SOUTH 9TH STREET

"Brotherly love" may explain why there are always at least three Micali brothers working together on 9th Street, selling seafood and produce. On weekends, away from the stock brokerage business is Michael Micali who joins brothers Joseph "Sonny," Anthony "Faci", and Vince "Dinky." Their roots are also in the Sicilian coastal village of Spadafora which makes them *paesani* to the Lucchesis, Giuntas, Anastasios, Giordanos, Lombardos, DeLucas and Darigos. Not surprisingly, the store's sign emphasizes fish, an ancestral occupation.

The recipe submitted here by Mike (who has no nickname) also reflects the brothers' "genetic tendency" towards seafood. It's a 9th Street favorite.

THE MICALI BROTHERS' CRABS & SPAGHETTI

"Figure on two crabs (or more) per adult," said Sonny.

Buy fresh, live crabs and ask the seller to remove the crabs' backs and any debris.

For 4, for example:

8   cleaned crabs   2 T   oil

2   cloves garlic, diced   1 lb. macaroni of choice

prepared tomato gravy/sauce

"Place crabs in frying pan that already sautéed the garlic in oil. Crabs' shells will be red when cooked; turn crabs as necessary. Meanwhile, cook macaroni according to instructions and place tomato sauce on stove to warm. Add crabs to prepared sauce and let sauce simmer on medium heat for about two hours." This is what Mike recommends— "you may want it to simmer less. Drain cooked macaroni. Then, add the 'crab gravy' to the macaroni and serve."

You'll love the taste to the gravy.

949 SOUTH 9TH STREET

John Gargano's father believed that his son's outside work on 9th Street was "too hard because of the weather." John hustles diligently at his produce stands at 9th and Carpenter Streets. To look at John, you are reminded of the "olden times" at the Market with the men who wore slouch hats and heavy moustaches and were in constant motion. He is a sentimental sight.

But, here's a secret: John has another side that's really sweet. He's outside, but look inside of his store, "The Italian Market Spice Company": "Babyboomers" and the pre-World War II generation will wonder where John found the candy factories that made the favorite confections of our youth. The "Mary Janes," the sugared "watermelon" slices, the licorice babies, the "penny candies" of our memories are here alongside of the dried fruits, packaged "trail mixes," snack nuts, spices and herbs.

John's Aunt Antoinette sits here inside and completes the picture of the old-fashioned candy store. Her recipe which follows uses some of the store's products which are naturally healthy.

AUNT ANTOINETTE GARGANO'S APPLE CAKE

In one bowl, mix together:

2 T	cinnamon	5 T	sugar
5	large red apples, peeled, and cored into 1/2" pieces		

In another bowl, mix:

3 C	flour	2 C	sugar
1 C	cooking oil	4	eggs
	juice of one orange	2 1/2 t	baking powder

"Grease and flour a large tube or Bundt pan and pour 1/2 of the batter into the pan; cover this batter with 1/2 apple mix. Pour remaining batter on top, then the other half of the apple mix. Lastly, sprinkle 1 C chopped walnuts on top."

"Bake at 350°F for 1 3/4 hours or until done."

Makes one big cake.

951 SOUTH 9TH STREET

Jay Zlotnick's one party on 9th Street who's always talking to another party about parties. Jay is the party man at 9th and Carpenter Streets, the only party who once was the only store on the street "from Christian to Washington Avenue that didn't sell food." His father, Herman began selling housewares and general merchandise at the Market in 1930. Jay continued with the latter goods and added health and beauty products. Now, his business is strictly "paper and party supplies…100%, non-stop shopping."

Jay's party lifestyle is however, fostered by a tribute to his father: "My father taught me never to try to 'get one on' a customer. Treat a customer right and they'll always come back." His fellow partiers include caterers, churches and other similar organizations who not just want to have a good time but have some good intentions behind the merriment. Jay claimed that his store is a "one-to-one basis store—like an old-fashioned store. We talk to our customers." Party-to-party communications.

CECILE STEIN ZLOTNICK'S CHOPPED LIVER

1 lb.	chicken or calves' livers	1 T	vegetable oil (or chicken fat)
4	yellow or white onions, diced	2	hard-boiled eggs
salt & pepper to taste			

"Sauté onions in oil until golden brown. Rinse off livers and brown with onions until done. Drain any drippings from pan. Cool livers. Chop up livers in one bowl; cut up eggs in another bowl, then add to chopped livers and mix. One option is to add some diced raw onion for a stronger flavor.

"This is an appetizer that serves 3 to 4 individuals, so serve it atop some lettuce or other garnish. Add sliced tomatoes and some assorted crackers." For a more decorative touch, Cecile recommends to place the chopped liver mix into a Jell-O mold.

813-21 CARPENTER STREET

After eating, gazzoza water was usually drunk to "settle" the stomach and aid in digestion. Gazzoza water-makers used machines to produce carbonation in liquids. That's what Chiara Imbesi had to teach her son, Anthony to use before he bought a lemon-lime soda franchise. He liked the soda called, "7-Up" and furthered its local distribution from his factory just off the 9th Street Market. In fact, the Imbesi family re-formulated 7-Up's ingredients here and in essence created a new soft drink, the "Un-Cola" in commercial advertizements.

A mason set green tile and bricks high above the garage to read "Home of 7-Up" to remind all of this drink's local roots.

No one will get *agita* from this cake recipe.

THE 7-UP CAKE

3 C	cake flour, sifted	1¹/₂ C	butter or margarine melted
2¹/₂ C	sugar	1 C	7-Up
4	eggs	1 t	baking powder

grated peel from one lemon and one lime

Preheat oven to 325°F.

With mixer, cream sugar and eggs together, then add the flour, butter (or margarine) and 7-Up. Mix to consistency. Lastly, fold in grated lemon and lime zest. Pour into greased and floured deep cake pan and bake for about one hour or until fork inserted in center comes out clean.

Ice or just sprinkle with 10X sugar.

WAS, NW CORNER, 9TH & CARPENTER STREETS

"Have food, will travel" seemed to be one saying among the Campo family members. Another saying had to be, "Go West!" because the Campos keep moving west all the time. First, the Campos went from Sicily to New Jersey; then, to 9th and Carpenter at the Market; then, as now, to West Philadelphia.

The Campo family was one of a few at the Market on 9th Street that brought what they grew or raised to be sold in Philadelphia. The Campos had a pig farm in New Jersey, while others had produce farms in the Garden State which they carried over the Delaware River. On 9th Street, the Campos slaughtered the pigs and sold their meats.

Today, the Campo name's only link with pork is in the deli meats that they use in their many ingenous sandwiches. In fact, the Campos keep Philadelphia's food heritage in sandwiches alive and flying around the world with their "mail-order" tastes of Philadelphia.

Denise Campo gets to create some interesting salads at the deli and she gladly (and quickly) arrived at this.

DENISE NANNI CAMPO'S PASTA SALAD

1 lb.	rigatoni	1	small red onion, diced
2	cloves garlic, diced	1 pkg. (8 oz.) frozen lima beans	
1	can Italian tuna, with oil	salt & pepper to taste	

"Cook rigatoni as directed, drain and set aside. Cook lima beans and place in bowl with tuna and oil, onion, garlic and macaroni. Season to taste." Serves four adults, hot or cold.

CABLE ADDRESS
MONTIRENO PHILADELPHIA

WHOLESALE DRUGGIST

ESTABLISHED 1901
TELEPHONE CONNECTIONS

MANUFACTURER & IMPORTER OF
ITALIAN PHARMACEUTICAL SPECIALTIES, DRUGGISTS
SUNDRIES, TABLE LUXURIES & PERFUMERY

GENERAL OFFICES
1000-02 S. 9TH STREET

LABORATORIES
900-02-04 CARPENTER ST.

Frank Sabelli humbly repeated a line since his birth: "My grandfather invented *senze*." These are the flavors that the druggist made for cooking and later, for those who made homemade alcohol. When you bought Nazareno Monticelli's "Flavors" you could make ordinary liquor into scotch, strega, or anisette. "Add a shot of the anisette flavor to a cup of espresso. Or add the creme de menthe over vanilla ice cream," said Frank's sister, Marie Sabelli Tomasso. Cavallier Monticelli, from Abruzzi, was educated in Italy and founded his business at 9th and Carpenter Streets in 1901. "The flavors were the only ones around," said grandson, Frank of the pre-extract products.

Frank and Marie also grew up in their father's business, "he used to be the largest Italian food importer in the city," called, "Gaetano Sabelli Food Importers" with their grandfather. *Senze* are no longer manufactured but anisette, almond, lemon or orange extracts can be used instead of vanilla in this recipe.

TEA BALLS

1 C	butter	1/2 C 4X sugar
1/2 t	extract flavoring	13/4 C flour
1/2 C	walnuts (crushed)	

Cream butter and sugar, then add remaining ingredients. Roll pieces of dough and make into little balls, about 1" wide.

Bake at 400°F for 10 minutes, then roll balls in 4X sugar as a coating.

1003 SOUTH 9TH STREET

Bob Georgette considers himself a simple man. "I'm just a plain sandwich maker," at 1003 South 9th Street. Humility leads to discretion: "Oh, I know a lot of stories about 9th Street, but..." he shook his head. He won't tell. Sal, the assistant manager laughed: "Oh, yeah...lots of stories."

Why do they tease me like this?

"No, I won't say anything," said Bob, still shaking his head. "And do we know stories about 9th Street!" Bob said, "Here." He's teasing me again, this time with a few slices of roast beef. "I can't say anything," he repeated. "Oh! Come on!" "Well, the President came in here while campaigning in '91. He asked for water. He paid for it." Well, Bob, anything more, like, "how long did Clinton stay in here?" "He stayed for about ten minutes." Bob then added, "He didn't say anything. 'just came in, asked for water, sat down, said nothing."

Anything more, Bob?

"I'm not a talker. But I'll tell you how to make roast beef."

ROAST BEEF FROM "GEORGE'S SANDWICHES"

6 lb.	eye roast	2-3	cloves garlic
1	large onion	salt & pepper	
1 qt. of water ("no more")			

"Preheat over at 350°F and cook roast beef in large pan with water and onion on sides. You might want to cut slits into the beef and insert with pieces of garlic.

The water and drippings make the beef gravy you'll need if making sandwiches."

1004-06-08 SOUTH 9TH STREET

Mary Rose Fante Cunningham is the only Fante left to carry on the tradition of service beyond her community. She was raised on 9th Street in a store above the Market where her parents, and "second parents," Emilia D'Orazio and Dominic Fante introduced her to food. "I still cook my gravy the same as my grandmother," said Mary Rose. She carries on a legacy of giving, just as her Uncle Dom who was a paragon of selflessness. Dom, at age 19 was given the responsibility of raising his five younger siblings *and* managing his store, "Fante's." While Boy Scout leader, a young Jimmy Tayoun was in his troop. "He'd be gone for days with the American Red Cross' disaster relief volunteers," recalled Mary Rose. Later, Dom Fante was one of the first appointed to the advisory board of Hall-Mercer. He sold his store in 1981.

Mary Rose's grandmother's Abruzzese recipe for meatballs is over one hundred years old and still a favorite at her home. It's an Italian standard.

MARY ROSE FANTE CUNNINGHAM'S GRANDMOTHER'S MEATBALLS

3 lbs.	beef, pork & veal mix	2	eggs
1 C	bread crumbs made by using stale bread, without crusts, dipped in milk and left to dry		
1/4 C	parsley, chopped	2	cloves garlic, mashed
1/2 C	locatelli cheese		salt & pepper to taste

"Combine all of the above ingredients. If the mix is too 'wet', add additional bread crumbs to make the ball-forming easier."

To fry:

Mary Rose uses "olive oil and shortening in equal portions in the pan. An average pan might call for about 2 T of each at first to sauté one small diced onion and 3 to 4 cloves of garlic until they turn golden. Then, add additional oil and shortening to level to fry the meatballs. Place meatballs into flavored oil-shortening in pan and turn as often to cook through. When meatballs are done, add to tomato gravy."

IT PAYS TO GO TO 9TH STREET...EVENTUALLY.

As Anthony L. Maglio told it, his grandfather had his hands full with his son, Anthony's uncle Tony. To avert the boy from mischief, the elder Maglio went to a butcher at the Italian Market and paid the butcher to hire his son, Tony. The boy would dutifully give his earnings from the butcherstore job to his father who then would continue to pay the butcher to keep the boy on the payroll.

After the service, with his butchering experience, Tony and his brothers Lou and John began making and selling sausage to the dry goods retailers at the Italian Market. There was, however, one condition—the Maglio's sausage could not be made with scraps, as the butchers on 9th Street did. At least this is what Anthony L. said. Thus, Maglio Sausage was born!

Anthony L. gave this recipe with the ease of one who knows his product well:

"MAGLIO'S SAUSAGE SURPRISE"

1 lb.	any sausage, cut in 1" pieces	2	large vidalia onions, cut
5	medium potatoes, cubed	2	green and 1 red bell peppers
3	cloves garlic, chopped	1/2	fresh sprig rosemary
	olive oil		salt & pepper to taste

"Pan fry the sausage in a deep skillet, then set aside. In a long, deep pyrex dish with about 1", of water, add the sausage and remaining ingredients and cover. Bake at 350°F for 1 1/2 hours. Remove the cover and let the potatoes and onions brown on broil for an additional 5 to 10 minutes." Anthony L. also suggested that a "mixture of 1 C Italian seasoned breadcrumbs and 1/2 C grated locatelli be sprinkled atop this dish."

Serves 4 to 6.

1005 SOUTH 9TH STREET

Triple A Poultry's sign actually volunteers this charitable owner to donate to church functions. Pete DeRito has a kind face and eyes, and obviously he's ready for giving. The sign's been outside for awhile, testifying to decades of selflessness.

Pete's mother, Toni Caliva DeRito, used to have her own luncheonette, "The Hungry Hut" for several years, baking homemade cornbread and making other "home-mades" like chili there. Ask Mrs. DeRito for a recipe and she stops to think: so many recipes to chose! "Please pick one, Mrs. DeRito." It's typical that she would think of a soup, something that warms the body, because of her own nurturing nature.

TONI CALIVA DeRITO'S ITALIAN BEEF SOUP

1/2 lb. (or more, if preferred) of a "big beef bone with chuck on it"

2-3	onions, diced	1 C	celery
1 C	carrots	4-5	cloves, garlic, diced
2 T	sugar	2 T	basil
1	large can, tomato paste or can of whole tomatoes, cut into pieces		
1 lb.	acini pepe macaroni, cooked and drained		salt & pepper to taste

"Fill a large pot with water to the half-way mark and let it come to a boil. Add bone with chuck beef and let cook until beef falls off bone. Add remaining ingredients, except for macaroni and let cook until vegetables are done. Lastly, add macaroni and stir. You can cook pieces of the beef to make this dish fuller.

Serve with a sprinkling of cheese on top."

Feeds 6 to 8 hungry adults.

1010 SOUTH 9TH STREET

Everytime that Joe Venuti was asked where he was born, the answer was always a different place. Officially, though not necessarily true, this genius with a violin was born 1 1/2 blocks from the 9th Street Market. His family then moved a few houses in from the Market while more pushcarts began to roll from Christian to 9th.

Venuti, the "Father of Jazz Violin," international star and jokester used to practice his classical violin lessons over his father's bakery until shortly before 1920 when he became a celebrity.

Forget about Joe's famous pranks, like the flour in the tuba or what he did to Roy Roger's horse, "Trigger" (don't ask!). Joe's father joined his fellow Sicilian bakers in the area and let his gifted son follow music instead of sugar. Joe's cousin, Florence De Maria also had her own bakery at 1010 South 9th Street, "The Pasticceria Catania" where the family "specialized in everything sweet," said Florence's daughter, Eleanor Gentile.

If you want to fiddle around in the kitchen with sugar and flour, the Venuti girls offer one of Joe's favorites.

DeMARIA'S ITALIAN CREAM PUFFS AND FILLING

The puffs: Makes 50 to 55 small ones.

1 C	water	1 C	flour, sifted
1/2 C	shortening	6 to 8 eggs	
pinch of salt			

"Boil water and shortening together to melt in saucepan and add flour gradually. Beat well until mixture forms a ball. Remove from heat, then add one egg at a time and beat well until the batter is smooth.

Preheat oven at 400°F. Using teaspoon, put dough onto lightly greased flat pan and space about 2" apart. Bake 20-25 minutes."

Italian Creme Filling makes about one pint:

3/4 C	sugar	1/3 C	flour
1 t	cornstarch	2 t	butter
3	egg yolks	2 C	milk
1 t	vanilla		

"Mix dry ingredients together, then put into a bowl and make a 'well.' Beat egg yolks aside and then drop into the 'well.' Slowly mix flour, eggs and milk together until smooth. Pour into pan and place on medium heat, stirring constantly so that bottom does not burn. Cook until mixture thickens and comes to a boil. Continue for two more minutes, stirring constantly. Remove from heat. Lastly, add vanilla and butter and then let cool. Cut cream puffs horizontally and insert with filling."

NOW, SW CORNER, 13TH & DICKINSON STREETS

Lovely "Aunt Connie" Ippolito DeAngelis glows as she says, "We are the largest seafood distributor, not just in this area, but all over." Her father, Giuseppe "Joe" Ippolito came to Philadelphia from the mountain town of Novara, Sicily and got a job with his wife's uncle at the 9th Street Market. The uncle owned "Darigo's Seafood" since about 1920. Joe sold fish for his uncle, handed his uncle the sales proceeds and was given a small salary. By 1929, Ippolito left the 9th Street Market and the uncle to sell his own fish, first as a neighborhood huckster, then in a store.

Now, five stores bear Joe's proud name. "We're the biggest, servicing the finest hotels and restaurants," said Aunt Connie. However, she also credits her nephew with the expansion of Ippolito's to include Samuel and Sons, and the largest seafood wholesale vending at the Food Distribution Center, the food emporium that was organized after ships ceased unloading at the Dock Street wharves.

One of Aunt Connie's many fishy recipes is here to try.

AUNT CONNIE'S MUSSELS IN WHITE SAUCE

5 lbs.	of white water mussels	1 C	blended oil (part olive oil)
6-8	cloves of garlic, chopped	1/3	stick butter
1	(8 oz.) jar, clam juice	1 1/2 C	water
1 1/4 C	dry white wine	1/4 C	fresh chopped parsley
1 T	dry basil		salt to taste
crushed red pepper to taste			

"Clean and debeard mussels. Sauté garlic in oil, until lightly golden, but not burned. Add all ingredients to pot, then the mussels. Cover tightly and cook over medium heat. Gently shake pot occasionally during cooking. Steam until all mussels are fully opened. Mussel sauce can be served over linguini, if desired, or with some crusty Italian bread. 'Bon Appetit,' said Aunt Connie."

WAS, 1014 SOUTH 9TH STREET

The Caltabiano poultry store on 9th Street has disappeared but the legend lives on every time the songs, "The Twist" and "Let's Twist Again" are played. Young Ernest Evans, a neighborhood resident who had spent a few years in produce with Tony Anastasio and Charlie "Hinks" went on in his stint at 9th Street with the Caltabiano family. In fact, Evans worked for about eight years in poultry until his employer, Henry Caltabiano decided that music was the best move for his employee. As Jerry Colt, Henry's son, related the facts, Evans used to hustle over the store's microphone. Henry's friend, Hank Ballard, a songwriter, had a song for the "B" side of his record and they matched Evans to it.

Sure, Henry made the first move, but it was Evans, later renamed, Chubby Checker, who made the moves in "The Twist" famous. Henry though, continued in the poultry business begun by his parents despite that he still managed Chubby's career through the 1960s. Chubby chickened out for a recipe but Marion Caltabiano, Henry's wife and Jerry's mother, provided this dish:

TURKEY SCALLOPINI WITH PROSCIUTTO & MOZZARELLA

8	turkey scallops	2 T	butter
1	clove crushed garlic		sprig of rosemary
8 slices each, prosciutto and mozzarella		3 T	sherry (or Marsala)
1/4 C	chicken or turkey stock		salt & pepper to taste

"Pound scallops between two pieces of waxed paper. Melt butter in pan and add turkey and garlic and cook until brown on both sides. Place prosciutto on top of scallops and add sherry, stock and rosemary. Cover and cook 10 minutes. Put in heat-proof dish, add cheese and pour liquid over scallops. Cover to let cheese melt."

Serves 4.

1013-19 SOUTH 9TH STREET

Mario Girardo is pleased to say, "I'm numbers 47 and 48." They are the reference numbers to his produce stands near Kimball and 9th Streets. The Girardo family has been weathering the unpredictable in "fair and blustery" outside on their stands since about 1916 with Mario's older uncles. Mario cited the typical day for a produce vendor: out of the house by 4:30 A.M. and working on the street until about 5 P.M., five days a week. His father, Jack, born in 1914 has been at his own stand, just up from Mario's, since about 1932. To date, he is the oldest produce huckster there. He saw the times when produce was purchased from ships on Dock Street or from the railroad cars near Oregon Avenue.

It's a hard life on the street.

Mario keeps warm in the winter with his firebarrel. His inner warmth is shown by his smile. He knows that he is the last of his family to have this occupation here.

Mario's mother, Rose Girardo gives this recipe that all of her children fall for.

ROSE CALTABIANO GIRARDO'S SEAFOOD LINGUINI

1¼ lb. shelled and deveined shrimp, cut into bite-size pieces

½ C	olive oil	1 lb.	scallops
½ C	onions, chopped	3½ C	chopped plum tomatoes
4	cloves garlic	1¼ C	mushrooms, thinly cut
½ C	anchovies, mashed	¼ C	capers
2 T	fresh basil	1¼ lb.	linguini
½ T	hot pepper (opt.)		fresh parsley to garnish
½ C	white wine		

"Cook pasta according to directions and set aside. In skillet, sauté onion, garlic, anchovies and basil in oil, then add seafood and cook on medium heat until shrimp turns pink. Pour mixture out to another dish. In same skillet, add tomatoes and cook them with capers, mushrooms and add basil and oil as needed for the 15 minutes of cooking time. Then add seafood mix to heat. Pour over cooked and drained linguini and serve."

This dish feeds four (very hungry) or six average individual appetites.

1019 SOUTH 9TH STREET

Mr. Harry Crimi, as President of the South Ninth Street Businessmen's Association for twenty years has had his share of elephants who loved the Market. When the circus came to Philadelphia, 9th Street merchants treated the animals to carrots and other vegetables. "This elephant was eatin' everything'!" said Carmen Lerro. But, "Oh, the stink!" Mr. Crimi's "elephant experiences" in the past were based more on honor than odor. In his twenty years of leadership (1972-1992), Mr. Crimi elevated the 9th Street Market to a political venue and brought national recognition to an otherwise neighborhood market.

Mr. Crimi escorted these "elephants": Gerald Ford, Ronald Reagan and George Bush through the market crowds where they courteously patronized some businessmen. Carmen Lerro said that Jerry Ford insisted on paying for his produce. The other "elephants" likewise left positive memories.

Elephants of all sorts aside, Mr. Crimi's organization of the 9th Street Festival brought out all of the party animals. Interspaced and spreading for four long

The D'Orazio Family's Linen Store at 1020-1022 S. 9th Street begun in the 1890s. Bernie Evantash later purchased the property.

blocks, bandstands of musicians or disc jockeys were set up for a variety of sounds to listen or to dance. Who can resist such a wonderful time amidst the food, the music and the excitement? Mr. Crimi brought out the spirit of the Market.

Thanks for the memories, Mr. Crimi!

And thank you, Mrs. Crimi for this memorable recipe.

ANTOINETTE CAPPUCCIO CRIMI'S
B O N Z E T T A !
(Sicilian-Style)

2-2¹/₂ lb. breast of veal	2 strips lean bacon
¹/₂ C diced onions	¹/₂ C diced celery
¹/₄ C parsley	2-3 C fresh hard bread
¹/₂ C locatelli	4-5 eggs, beaten
salt and pepper to taste	

"Sauté bacon with onions. Then add celery and parsley and mix. In a bowl, cube the bread. Add sautéed mix and remaining ingredients, using the eggs as a binder. Stuff into veal pocket and place into pan. Set oven on broil and cook for about 2 hours at 350°F or until veal is tender."

1021-27 SOUTH 9TH STREET

Carmen Lerro is cute and bluntly honest. The 9th Street Italian Market is in his blood, having worked the street from an early age. His great-grandfather, grandfather and father depended on business from the street for survival but they lived well. Carmen said that Willie Mosconi and Minnesota "Fats" used to play billiards in his grandfather's basement on 9th Street. "It was like nothin', then." Carmen has some memories: "My grandfather used to tell me to go and put sawdust on the floor of the store in the old days when 9th Street was really crowded. You know, basically, the sawdust was for the blood of the animals but also for the old ladies who would go to the bathroom right there in the store while they were waiting to order meat." He repeated, "They'd go to the bathroom right there in the store!" Carmen then asked me if I have anything written on the "hustlin'" "You know what hustlin's for...to get attention to your stand." Carmen has a rhythmic bunch of "hustlin's":

"Every bean with a bang and every bang with a bean."

"Cheap, cheap, cheap, all the meat you wanna eat!"

"If you can beat it, I'll eat it!"

"Put it on the pot, let it get hot. Put it on the grill, give it a thrill."

"You have fun with 'em," Carmen said. "I made up my own lines and got some from relatives." I then hear a word that sounds phonetically like, "immini!" from "Popeye" next to Carmen. Carmen translated: "'How many?' is what 'Popeye's' saying." Marie and Frankie Messina add to the "music" at the Market.

Carmen's hustlings remind me of the recipes that Barbara Moses submitted. Barbara's now the principal of the Philadelphia Mennonite High School but previously worked for the School District of Philadelphia. We wrote a program on the 9th Street Market which garnered Barbara an award. She's a frequent shopper on 9th Street: "I've always had a pleasant experience there...It's the only place where I don't mind the crowds." Barbara's recipes call for meat and vegetables together in these traditional side dishes.

BARBARA MOSES' COLLARDS

2-3 lbs. collard greens	4-5 strips (or more) bacon
pinch of sugar	seasoned salt to taste
regular salt & black pepper	

"Wash collards good," said Barbara, "then cut them into small pieces. In a deep pot, cook the cut strips of bacon until golden but not crisp. Add about 1½ to 2 quarts of water to pot to cover collards. Boil down the greens, then add seasoned salt, pepper, sugar and salt. Bring temperature down and let simmer until done."

BARBARA MOSES' STRING BEANS

2 lbs. fresh string beans	1 lb. turkey neck bones
seasoned salt to taste	regular salt & pepper

"Wash string beans and cut ends. Snap the beans in halves or in thirds and set aside. In a large pot, boil turkey neck bones in water with some regular salt to create a broth. When meat on bones is cooked, add beans and more water and boil on high heat. When beans are cooked, but not limp, turn heat down and add seasoned salt, pepper and regular salt, if necessary."

This should serve four hungry adults with ample helpings.

SOLD ESPECIALLY AT 1036 SOUTH 9TH STREET

Remember the song, "Yankee Doodle"? He went to town, riding on a pony. Then, he stuck a feather in his cap and for no other reason than to rhyme "called it, 'macaroni.'"

Well, a gentleman who achieved his American dream near 9th Street rightfully can be called, "Mr. Macaroni" because his pasta from the Italian Market neighborhood is everywhere in the U.S. and in most places in the world. Mr. Luke Marano, the grandson of pioneering immigrant Antonio owns what is possibly the largest macaroni production company in the U.S. He was Chair of the National Pasta Association in 1996 and headed the First World Pasta Congress in Rome, Italy.

You've eaten his pasta if you ate Campbell or Lipton Soups, Ramen Noodles, Ronzoni and Conte Luna Macaroni. It's everywhere! The Philadelphia Macaroni Company has been in the neighborhood since about 1914 and with Mr. Marano's acumen has extended to the most remote parts of the country. "The pasta business has given me the opportunity to go throughout the world," said the man whose macaroni is all over the world. Now, what had been an "Italian" food is universal, thanks to gentlemen like Mr. Marano.

As a salute to Mr. Marano's roots near Naples comes this dish, given by permission of Conte Luna:

NEAPOLITAN BOW TIE PASTA WITH VODKA CREAM SAUCE

12 oz.	Conta Luna Egg Bow Ties		4	C heavy cream
3	garlic cloves, minced		2 C	Parmesan cheese
2	shallots, minced		3 oz.	smoked salmon
2 T	cooking oil		2 oz.	vodka
2 t	chives		2 C	white wine
salt & pepper to taste				

Cook macaroni according to directions. Drain. Sauté garlic and shallots in oil until done but not brown. Then add vodka and white wine and simmer. Add cream on same temperature and continue to stir. Gradually stir in cheese and continue to stir. Lastly, add salmon and chives. Serves 6 adults as a warm dish.

An *"ancora"* from Mr. Marano!

PESTO ROTINI SALAD WITH PROSCIUTTO

1	lb. Conte Luna Rotini		1 C	cherry tomatoes, halved
2	small yellow squash, cut into 1/4" half circles		3 oz.	prosciutto, cut into thin strips
2 C	green beans in 1" pieces		4 oz.	plain yogurt
7 oz.	pesto (1/2 C)		1/2 C	toasted walnuts
1 T	red wine vinegar		salt & pepper (ground black) to taste	

Cook and drain macaroni. In a large bowl, combine cooled macaroni and remaining ingredients. Serves 8 as a cold salad.

RAN AROUND WASHINGTON AVENUE AND SOUTH 9TH STREET

The title, "Rocky," described the filming of the movie at 9th Street Market more than the story of a would-be prizefighter from the rough. Locals at the Market didn't respond well to Stallone. "Nobody told us what was going on. We thought someone was making a home movie," said Mario Girardo. Another take: "No one know who he (Stallone) was then," explained Carmen Lerro. "We saw this guy running and thought that he stole somethin'."

Sylvester Stallone, sans fruit on face, as "Rocky" in 1974. (Photo was gift to Pip DeLuca from Frank Palumbo, Sr.)

Chuckie Amoroso had his own stand on 9th Street then. (He's now retired.) Chuckie saw Stallone running up 9th and tossed him a piece of fruit. "Rocky" caught the fruit and it stayed in the film. Then, "Rocky" threw the fruit to someone else—"Oh, NO!"

Smash!

Then, retaliation: the "mysterious flying fruit" that hit "Rocky" hard on the side of his face. Worse happened on Washington Avenue—rotten produce pelted at the future "Rambo" for half a block!

There was a lot of film on the editing floor...

Such a memorable man and times deserve this popular Sicilian dish that feeds one "Rocky" or four to six average individuals.

SICILIAN BLOOD ORANGE SALAD

5-6	blood oranges, or regular ones from Florida, peeled and halved		
1/4 C	extra virgin olive oil	1 C	black olives, pitted
6	anchovies, cut in half	1/2 C	red onion, diced
1 T	ground black pepper		salt to taste

Combine all ingredients together and serve. *A knock-out!*

115

A ONE-TIME A YEAR TREAT ON 9TH STREET

Surprises abound at the Italian Market festival each year when outside vendors are invited to participate in the five-hour event. There is a little of something for everyone. Got the "woolies" for something spicey? 9th Street's got it. Chinese? It's here, too. Now, how about something nice and sweet—there it is: Termini Brothers Gold Medal Pastry!

This classy bakery makes an annual appearance on 9th Street to remind us that the South Philadelphia institution can be eaten on this occasion of rowdiness. Amidst the excitement in the greasepole climbing and the dance bands, there are people eating the delicious, award-winning cannoli, the cream puffs, the cookies and sfogliatelli.

Termini Brothers is not limited to the sugarfilled, however. Here is Vince's contribution, a safe exit from his business.

TERMINI'S PIZZA RUSTICA

Pie Crust:

2 C	flour	3 t	shortening
2/3 t	baking powder	1	egg
1/3 t	salt	1/2 C	ice cold water

"Sift the dry ingredients together. Blend the shortening into the sifted flour with a fork. Mix the egg with the cold water. Add to the flour and mix until a ball is formed. Refrigerate."

Filling:

8 oz.	dried sausage or pepperoni, diced	3/4 lb.	fresh sausage meat, browned lightly in 1 T water
2	hard-boiled eggs, diced	4 oz.	salami, diced
8 oz.	mozzarella, diced	1 lb.	"fresh" cheese
2 oz.	ham, diced	4 oz.	prosciutto, chopped
2	eggs	1 T	grated romano cheese
dash of salt			

"Combine the fresh cheese, salt and romano cheese, while adding two eggs, one at a time, beating after each with a wooden spoon. Add the sausage" and other meats and cheeses and mix well.

"Prepare the pastry. Roll out and line a 10" deep pie pan with the pastry. Prick dough with fork. Sprinkle bottom with a little flour. Pour mixture into a lined pie pan and cover with the top pie crust. Trim, leaving about 1/2" overhang. Fold dough under and back to flute. Cut slits in pie and bake in preheated oven at 400°F for 15 minutes, then 45 minutes at 325°F."

116

1143 SOUTH 9TH STREET

Connie Tartaglia swears that she can't cook! Can you imagine someone with the name of Connie Villari Tartaglia claiming she's uncomfortable in the kitchen! Yet, her husband, "Joe Brown" loves this dish. "Joe Brown" is Pip DeLuca's vice president in the South Ninth Street Curb Market Association, a true "9th Streeter" with a creative mind and heart of gold. Joe had the idea of stringing electric lights across 9th Street in red, white and green. For Christmas of 1998, he chose all white.

Joe's life has been on 9th Street since he was a child. He said that his grandfather had a stand on 9th Street in the 1930s. Joe brought Connie there, then their boys, Frank and Joe who also found inspiration in the culture of the Market. Connie is very nonchalant about the life of a 9th Street businessperson: "I don't cook." Sure, Connie. Joe's favorite dish was taught to Connie by her mother who was taught to make it by Connie's father, Frank.

Joe knows this recipe by memory—that's how much he enjoys this dish. ("I can't believe he gave it to you!" said his wife.) This is how Joe likes this to be cooked.

CONNIE'S CHICKEN & PEAS WITH SPAGHETTI

4 lbs. chicken legs and thighs, with skin on (the way Joe likes)

1	can sweet peas, with water	3 C	cooking oil
1 lb.	spaghetti	1	onion, diced

salt & pepper to taste

—— Optional ——

1 C	mushrooms	1 C	white wine

not the way Joe likes it, but it's the way Connie's mother prefers

Cook spaghetti as directed and set aside.

"In a large skillet, pour the oil and place on low heat. Add parts of chicken and let cook for one hour. Then add onion, peas and water from peas and cook with chicken for another hour. "I like to let it cook long," said Connie. Check chicken and remove when it begins to fall apart. Pour atop spaghetti and serve."

Serves about four individuals.

1146 SOUTH 9TH STREET

The Italian Market has its own royalty, like Duke Capocci, Kaiser DeLuca, a few queens here and there, but this Caesar is the real gentleman. Mr. and Mrs. DiCrecchio appropriately named their distinguished-looking son, "Caesar," whose fruit baskets make him widely known. People from all over the U.S. contact Caesar for his beautiful baskets which use, coincidentally, some Rosa products among other delicious ones.

The food business brought Caesar's family to the 9th Street Market in the 1930s. His grandmother brought produce from their farm in Delaware County to sell in the city. Caesar's son is a manager at the Food Distribution Center, the fourth generation involved with food in Philly. In his store, Caesar does a little creative cooking aside from his artistic fruit baskets, as this recipe shows. Warning: they're hot!

CAESAR'S ITALIAN SNACK: DRIED RED PEPPERS

2 lbs. or more long, hot, red peppers ("They have to be red.")

cooking oil to fill deep fryer

This is not a ready-snack: "it'll take 3 to 4 weeks to get maximum results in the taste."

Caesar places his long hots "on a pan and then in an oven for about 1 minute over a low temperature. Do this every day for three or four weeks until the long hots are dry as a bone. Then break off the stems and drop the dried long hots into the deep fryer for just a few seconds." Let them dry on paper towels. "Eat them like potato chips," said Caesar, "They're delicious." They must be: "Joe Brown" Tartaglia never passes Caesar's offers of the long hots.

WAS AT 1154 SOUTH 9TH STREET

The culture of the 9th Street Italian Market created traditions within families.

JoAnn Yerkov, daughter of Theresa Parisi recalled her mother's life at 1154 South 9th Street: "There was no such thing as planning an activity on a Saturday. It was just never heard of because that was the busiest day of all and we knew better than to disrespect their [grandparents'] way." JoAnn's grandparents were John and Josephine Parisi whose great love for each other was passed on to their children. "We all were lucky to share with one another," said JoAnn. "Dad Parisi" would sell his produce wholesale to stores and restaurants while "Mom Parisi" handled the retail part of the business with the kids closeby.

Three or four produce stands kept the Parisi family tight: "Nothing came before the fact that each of us had to do their share with Mom and Dad...This is how it was," said JoAnn, matter-of-factly. No one minded the limitations of the 9th Street culture because the families created their own amusements, usually around food. Mom Parisi's holiday recipe for St. Joseph's Day Cake was memorialized in writing by her namesake granddaughter, JoAnn, who wanted to keep her tradition.

JOSEPHINE PARISI'S ST. JOSEPH'S DAY CAKES

2 T	sugar	2 lbs.	flour
1 C	raisins	2	eggs, beaten
1 pkg.	yeast	1 t	vanilla
dash of salt		1½-2 C warm water	

"Soak raisins in warm water and set aside. Dissolve yeast according to directions. Combine ingredients, including yeast in a large bowl. Stir to a consistency of batter. Prepare a large frying pan to be hot and oiled. Spoon batter into frying pan and turn over, as a pancake, when one side is cooked. If the cakes are too oily, let them dry on a paper towel. Sprinkle granulated sugar on top and eat hot or cooled."

CHILDHOOD SPENT SHOPPING ON SOUTH 9TH STREET

Mario Lanza and food.
Food and Mario Lanza.

It's impossible to discuss his life without a reference to food.

Mario Lanza, né, Alfredo Cocozza, faced food daily with his grandparents' grocery store. His aunt, Julia Alioto and her husband also had one at 9th and Catharine Streets. And the great tenor shopped the 9th Street Market regularly with his mother as a child in the 1920s. The Cocozzo family, with the Lanza's, Mario's mother's family, lived two blocks east of the Market on Christian where music combined with food.

Maria Lanza Cocozza, Mario's mother, was a fine cook who spoiled her talented son with her imaginative recipes such as the one submitted here, a Cocozza family favorite.

Tenor Mario Lanza and wife, Betty, cooking together. (Photo courtesy, Mario Lanza Museum, Philadelphia)

MARIO LANZA'S MOTHER'S PIZZA Di RICOTTA
(As sweet as Mario's voice.)

5 lbs.	ricotta	3 lbs.	parmesan or locatelli
16	eggs		(unsalted and grated)
5 C	sugar	1/2 t	nutmeg

juice and zest of 1 orange and 1 lemon

"Combine cheeses in a large bowl. Gradually add eggs while stirring. Then add the sugar, nutmeg, juices and zests and stir to consistency."

Dough:

1 lb.	flour		pinch of salt
3 T	sugar	4	eggs
3 T	peanut oil (preferred by Mrs. Cocozza over vegetable oil)		

zest of 1 lemon

"Mix all ingredients together to form a soft dough. Knead well. Roll out dough and place in a large buttered pan that is at least 3", deep and 10" wide. Let dough over the brim of pan to about 1/2". Keep excess dough aside. Spoon cheese/egg mixture atop of dough. With extra dough, cut strips and lay crisscross atop mixture. Bake in preheated oven at 325°F for 2 1/2 to 3 hours."

Serve warm like a deep-dish pizza. Serves 6-8 adults.

1151 SOUTH 9TH STREET

Yo, Chris Marchando LaRocca!

How ya doing down there at 1151 South 9th Street?

There's pretty Chris selling "lots of pots and dishes" along with a variety of other things in her mostly kitchen variety store. "This is my husband's whole life—I just go along for the ride." Dominic LaRocca was born and raised at 9th and Fitzwater Streets, became a waiter at Palumbo's and met Chris while she was visiting the city. Dominic then married the nice, pretty, Italian girl from Pittsburgh. Likewise, Chris learned that Italians at the Market were different and that the Market was different for other Italians. She and Dominic took a chance on a store where people waited at 7 A.M. for the doors to open.

Since then, Chris and Dominic's store on 9th Street has never been more diversified with the lottery number, newfangled kitchen gadgets and electronics and the cutest novelties sold next to the stainless steel cookware, decorative spaghetti bowls and demitasse sets.

Chris has it all in this ecletic store where even John Gotti was charmed to make a buy...in cash.

Chris loves to cook and gives this omelet her own signature style of a little of this and a little of that to make an unusual, but healthy meal.

OMELET WITH VARIETY a la CHRIS LAROCCA

2 lbs. zucchini ("thin ones") sliced 1" thick

1/2-1 C diced onions	2 T	blended oil
1 clove garlic, diced	3-4	medium Jersey tomatoes
2 T basil	3	eggs, beaten
4 T locatelli cheese, grated	salt & pepper to taste	

"Sauté zucchini with onions and garlic until onions are carmelized. Place slices of tomatoes (in circle shapes) and basil on top and let simmer over medium heat until tomatoes are soft. Then add eggs and cheese, pouring mixture on top. Let it cook like an omelet. Add more grated cheese and basil on top, if desired."

WAS AT 1168 SOUTH 9TH STREET

The Market is filled with all types of sounds, some human, some aboriginal and some from unseen sources. The most mellifluous sound on 9th Street however, comes from the south end of the Market from butcher Frank Munafo who after fifty years just closed his store in order to bring more of his operatic voice to the masses.

Frank is a success as a tenor and has a talent in the kitchen as well. Sometimes he offers recipes to local restaurants.

No need to sing like Frank for your supper, just fix one of Frank's delicious dishes.

FRANK MUNAFO'S MEDITERRANEAN STEW

1 lb. Chilean sea bass (or scrod or cod)

1/2 C diced onions	2 T	oil
1/2 lb. Roma (plum) tomatoes, skinned	1/4 C	parsley, chopped
1/2 to 3/4 C white wine		

Frank's easy recipe calls for the fish fillets. "Sauté onion in oil in a deep pan over medium heat. Add parsley, then the tomatoes and gradually add white wine and simmer. Add water to mix to prevent evaporation and add fish last. Continue to simmer."

"Meanwhile, prepare some basmati rice. When fish stew is finished, drizzle virgin olive oil on top and then pour over the rice. Only use salt and pepper if you must."

NW Corner, Federal & South 9th Street

Alexander "Jules" Cardelli's shop, "Reliable Meats" has a certain something.

Maybe it's the way that the building tilts to let the sun illuminate the wide L-shaped counters through large windows on the east and south sides. One passes by and sees men sipping coffee and talking inside while Mr. Cardelli deftly cuts his meat. "I show you the meat, then I grind it for you," he said so gently. He's been butchering since 1934 when his uncle taught him the trade. "I ended up here [on 9th Street] after the service because I lived around the block at 10th and Ellsworth." The windows are inviting: he has a nice smile for those looking through them. Come through the door and ask him, "What do you do that's different, Mr. Cardelli?" His answer: "I make sausage for the street vendors around town." He's on the shy side. Work is his life.

At home, his sister looks after him, but it's a veritable social scene there, too, especially the way that Josephine cooks. This is one of her many recipes that few can turn away from.

JOSEPHINE CARDELLI BERNIER'S STUFFED ROAST PORK

6-8 lb.	center cut pork		6	slices prosciutto
2-3	roasted peppers (from jar)		6	slices soprasotta
1/3 C	parmesan cheese, grated		1/4 C	fresh parsley
3-4	garlic cloves, diced		2-3 T	rosemary
salt & pepper			1 C	spinach

Mrs. Bernier said to ask the butcher to "butterfly" the pork. With the pork open, lay down the pieces of prosciutto and soprasotta, then the peppers, cheese and spinach. Some garlic pieces can be placed inside—this is up to the cook and eaters. Some garlic pieces can be inserted into slits made into the pork after it has been rolled up and tied with a butcher cord. After tying the pork, brown it in the pan on high heat; then, place it in an open pan with about 1" of water. Sprinkle rosemary, salt and pepper on top and cook in oven at 325°F for about 1 1/2 hours uncovered and 2-3 hours covered. A little butter on top aids in the browning, she said.

1205 South 9th Street

Speaking of twists, there's a pretzel connection to 9th Street. "I grew up in this business...it was here before I was born," said Blanche Nacchio of Federal Pretzel Company. Her father, Joseph, was a baker in Salerno and came to the U.S. just before World War I, making some of the most sought-after bread in the area.

Herbert Hoover, then of the U.S. Department of Agriculture, sent agents to check reports if Joe was using more wheat flour during war-time rationing. Joe wasn't.

Some years later unfortunately, Joe died and his widow and older children chanced to try baking pretzels instead of bread and rolls in their South Philadelphia neighborhood. "They do the regular pretzel shape and plaits," said Blanche. Back in 1949, a relative told her to go to 9th Street, at the Market and meet this war veteran, a nice bachelor named Paul at his store at 9th, below Federal Street. A short time later, she became Mrs. Paul Marella. They're still in love.

Thinking of her "sweetie," Paul, Blanche gives this confection. "Oh," she added, "Federal does heart-shaped pretzels, too!"

BLANCHE MARELLA'S STUFFALI

8	egg yolks	1/2 t	baking powder
1 C	flour		pinch of salt
	jimmies	1/2 C	honey

"Make a dough with the egg yolks, flour, baking powder and salt. Place dough on a floured board and roll out into 1/4" wide and 1/2" cut wide pieces. "They grow," said Blanche. Drop pieces of dough into a deep fryer and then drain dough pieces on paper towel. When dried, place dough pieces into a bowl in which honey has been heated and coat pieces with honey. Add jimmies.

"It's really a Christmas dish. It's a treat!"

Note: Many ladies arrange the stuffali in clusters to form a "wreath" of stuffali balls and then add some other edible decorations, such as candies or colored sprinkles.

EATEN AT 1200 BLOCK SOUTH 9TH STREET

The Vilotti-Pisanelli Bakery's bread is, unknowingly, very well-known, well-eaten and well-digested. It's at Pat's Steaks and Geno's Steaks, eaten by thousands, maybe over 25,000 people on some weeks. Almost everyone has eaten this bread, without realizing its name. U.S. presidents ate Vilotti-Pisanelli's, as did Oprah, prizefighters, major (and minor) celebrities, sports figures and regular people.

Vilotti-Pisanelli's bread's versatility goes from fast-food to more serious dining however. Nick Marinelli was the founder of the small bakery that is older than the 9th Street Market: in 1898, he started baking the same as in his native

Abruzzi. Sometime in the late 1940s, Mr. John Taxin, the owner of Bookbinder's Restaurant, contacted Nick and asked if he could produce a similar type of dinner roll that he ate on his trip in France. Voilá! Marinelli's creation has since been exclusively served as the Bookbinder Dinner Roll.

V-P's present owner, an oven-warm gentleman named Dan Pisanelli, inherited his father, Dan, Sr.'s love of bread, but not his skill for cooking. "What did Daddy stuff in his bread?" he asked his sister.

From Dan's heart, excuse, hearth to yours, here's his father's recipe that's great for a fast meal:

DAN'S "STUFFED BREAD"

1 loaf French or "fat" Italian bread that's 12 to 18" long

1/2 lb. sliced pepperoni

1/2 lb. sausage bits (cooked & diced)

2 to 3 hard boiled eggs, cut up

1/4 lb. each of sliced mozzarella, provolone and sliced capicola

Cut loaf horizontally leaving about 1/4 of the top of the loaf off. "The juices from the meats will lubricate the bread," said Dan. Add no oil. "Scoop out the inside of the bread and line the bottom and sides with the meats, cheeses and egg pieces. Wrap the loaf in aluminum foil and bake low at about 250°F in the oven for about 15 minutes or until the cheeses melt."

BOTH ON 1200 BLOCK OF SOUTH 9TH STREET

Real Philadelphians laugh at the tourists who want the "Philly cheesesteak," that international food that is also known as just plain "steak sandwich" or the "Philly steak."

It's the classic fast-food.

The traditional sandwich however, is the product made exactly in 1930 as Pasquale "Pat" Olivieri, its inventor, made it: steak and onions on an Italian (read it: Vilotti-Pisanelli) roll.

That's it!

Let the thinly-sliced rib-eye steak and fried onions saturate the bread with its juices. Then eat it. Now, you've just eaten an original Philadelphia steak sandwich!

At Pat's Steaks, the home of the steak sandwich, the operation is still family-owned and run. The shop sits on a triangular-shaped "block" that once inspired other steak houses to open across, below and above it. There was "Mike and Carol's Steaks," "Jim's," "Joe's" and a "Pat's Steaks" where one can eat inside. (No way!), then "Geno's," making this area the "Steak House Haven of the World!" "Pat's" and "Geno's" now remain as all-time favorites. In both steak shops, patrons are urged to specify the cheese type, if they must have the cheesesteak that "outsiders" promote.

Here's how to make your own, the real Philly Steak Sandwich.

THE ORIGINAL PHILLY STEAK SANDWICH

Mr. Joseph Vento of Geno's Steaks recommends 4 to 8 ozs. of very good or "prime" rib-eye steak per sandwich.

3 to 4 medium onions, diced

cooking oil of your choice (I'm keeping "Pat's" and "Geno's" brands a secret!)

salt and pepper to taste

fresh Italian "steak" or "hoagie" rolls

Fry steaks and onions together in the oil with salt and pepper. Use oil as needed, judging how the onions and beef will absorb it. Keep drippings. Load everything in your fresh roll. Wait until drippings soak into the bread well and then eat it.

1200 BLOCK SOUTH 9TH STREET OR, WHERE PASSYUNK AVENUE CROSSES SOUTH 9TH STREET

One has to love the way that Sam Agresta has a knack for attracting the simplest things at the 9th Street Italian Market. He reminds 9th Street regulars about the hospital guerney that doubles as a produce stand. But there are also the stores that put café umbrellas up under the awnings, the "subjective art" that is really red and green paint droppings on the pavements and the dozen or so "businesses" that have no signs to identify them. Only on 9th Street at the Italian Market!

Sammy finds the simple and turns them into the positive, like his cooking. "I can't cook," he said after we talked for a few hours. But, he can make this antipasto, "that is the best!" which "I only make for people who are related to me, people I like and people I love." It's so simple, too!

125

SAM AGRESTA'S ANTIPASTO

The day before combine:

1	("#10") can of artichokes, cut in half	1	clove garlic, chopped
1 t	salt	1/2 t	black pepper
2 t	garlic powder	4 oz.	olive oil
4 oz.	red wine vinegar		

Let everything marinate overnight.

The next day, in a large dish, arrange artichokes with:

6   or more roasted peppers
1/2 lb. cubed sharp provolone
1 C   marinated mushrooms
1 C   each, black pitted & green olives
1/2 lb. each, sliced soprasata and prosciutto, ("rolled up")

Sam suggested to be creative with your ingredients—make a dish look nice by arranging the ingredients by color or shape.

You can use the "juice" that the artichokes soaked in as a dressing on top of the cheese and meats or just drip some olive oil and balsamic vinegar on to "liven up" the meats.

SOUTH 9TH STREET AT

WHARTON ST. & PASSYUNK AVENUE

"Avec ou non?" "Excusez moi?" The Italian Market has a French flavor at the far south end of 9th Street. Watch Frank Olivieri's wrist make a graceful flip of the steak and onions on the grill and you'll notice a serious student of French cuisine. "I had six years of French. I even read recipes in French! Now look where it got me: I'm at Pat's Steaks!"

Frank is the son of Pat's Steaks' owner, Frank, Sr., and grandnephew of the famous Philly Steak Sandwich's inventor, Pasquale "Pat" Olivieri who, by a fluke, fried some thinly sliced beef on a grill with oil and onions and put it in a small loaf of Italian bread.

It was 1930.

Pat was tired of eating hot dogs. As Frank, Jr. would say, "La remnant est la histoire!"

Here's another Olivieri food creation:

FRANKIE'S GNOCCHI WITH ROSÉ CRAB SAUCE

2 T	extra virgin olive oil	2	cloves minced garlic
2 cans (16 oz.) tomatoes		1/2 lb.	jumbo lump crab meat
2 C	heavy whipping cream		("The best you can buy.")
1 lb.	gnocchi	salt & pepper to taste	

Cook gnocchi as directed and drain.

"In a 2-3 quart pot, sauté garlic in oil. Add tomatoes and cook for 15 minutes on low to medium heat. Then add cream and crab meat and cook an additional 10 minutes on same temperature. Salt and pepper to taste. Pour over gnocchi and toss. Garnish with fresh basil." Serves four.

THE ITALIAN MARKET AS THE FIELD STUDY

Rosario (Russell) and Accursia (Mary) Morello weren't "city people" in western Sicily and never intended their children to be "city people" either. For over six decades, three of their grandchildren and five great-grandchildren in four businesses have been involved in services and products at the Italian Market. "To live this fascinating experience by 9th Street makes my work as a criminologist and historian more immeasurably valuable," said their great-granddaughter.

Celeste as historian wrote the first book on the Italian Market neighborhood in *Beyond History: The Times & Peoples of St. Paul's Roman Catholic Church, 1843-1993* (Jefferies & Manz, 1992), a Master's thesis, a few scholarly papers on the neighborhood's crime history and school programs. And of the twenty-two (22) historical markers she worked with the Pennsylvania Historical & Museum Commission to erect, six are in the "Little Italy" community, not including the "Palumbo" marker which she also is responsible for.

To "escape" from the stress in the criminological work, Celeste gives the "Italian Market Tours" which are the only food tours in Philadelphia honored by *Food & Wine*, The Restaurant School, The Atwater Kent Museum (The History Museum of Philadelphia), The Society of FoodService Management, Associated Press, among others.

"These are two recipes that hail from western Sicily which men and women in my family have been making for almost 120 years here in the U.S."

"'NZUOIGGHIU"
(A marinade for meat or fish)

2	cloves garlic, mashed	1/2 C	fresh mint, chopped
1/3 C	olive oil	1/2 C	wine vinegar or better,
salt & pepper to taste		1/2 C	lemon juice

This is best made with a mortar and pestle. Combine all ingredients to a consistency and dab on a steak or fish on the grill.

SICILIAN BEEF SALAD

2 lbs. or more, steak or beef roast that was cooked, cooled and cubed into small pieces

1/2 C	onion, diced	1/2 C celery and celery leaves, diced
1 C	pitted Sicilian olives	"dashes" of garlic, onion and celery salts
1/2 C	red wine vinegar	salt & pepper to taste
1/2 C	olive oil	

Let beef marinate in oil and vinegar for about 1 hour before adding other ingredients. Serve cold as an entreé.

EATEN & SOLD ALL OVER SOUTH 9TH STREET

The pride of the Italian American community in Philadelphia used to be when the Italian Grocers Association had their formals at the Ben Franklin Hotel. There, anyone of Italian ancestry who was in the food industry would be able to meet and to socialize with any other businessman of his class within one hundred miles of the city.

One of Giacomo (Jack) Foti's many Italian Grocers of Philadelphia formals, c. 1935.

(Photo by Bellino, courtesy of Rosa Foods, Inc.)

A vestige of these times is the Rosa Food Products. It may be *the* oldest, or one of the oldest Italian food businesses in the Philadelphia area. It began in 1903 and continues today. Named after his wife, Rosa, Giacomo "Jack" Foti rose to wholesale importer from a simple street huckster at 13th and Federal Streets. Leonardo Foti, his son, continued the business, then passed it on to his son, Jack. Today, Jack manages his grandparents' legacy, selling an impressive line of imported Italian foods which are found in most stores at the 9th Street Market where "Rosa Food Products" has been a tradition.

Jack's wife, Mary Storniolo Foti, has the same ancestral roots as her husband in Riposto, Sicily and gives not one, but two traditional recipes that are made extra delicious with Rosa Foods.

MARY FOTI'S PENNE LISCI WITH ZUCCHINI

1 lb. penne lisci	1/4-1/2 C Rosa Olive Oil
2-3 lbs.zucchini, washed and cut in circles	
grated parmesan or romano cheese	

"Fry zucchini in olive oil until tender but not limp. Cook and drain macaroni and set aside. Then, take zucchini with oil and pour over macaroni. No need to season further—the cheese will satisfy the taste." Serves four.

"Ancora, Mary!"

ASPARAGUS TIPS a la MARY FOTI

1 lb. spaghetti	3-4 C asparagus tips
1 large can Rosa Plum Tomatoes	grated cheese to taste

"Cook and drain macaroni as directed and set aside. Pour can of tomatoes into pot and place on medium to high heat. Cut tomatoes into pieces and add asparagus tips to cook for about 15 minutes. When heated, remove from stove and pour over macaroni."

Serves four.

NOT QUITE A FINALE.

One last, true 9th Street Italian Market story to close ...

One day, Nick Ingenito was in a hurry, walking towards 9th and Christian Streets, but not too much in a hurry to talk to our man, Charlie "Hinks." Nick was carrying a small plastic bag on which was the name of one of the Jersey casinos. "Do you know who this is?" Nick asked as he pointed to the bag. Charlie shook his head. "I have to drop 'him' (in the bag) off—the first family didn't want 'him.' Now I have to ask these other ones if they want 'him.'"

The "him" was in cremated form.

Nick was trying to find someone to claim these remains. At the least, he was hoping that someone would be able to provide a proper send-off or way to say "goodbye." Charlie "Hinks" was speechless. No one at the Italian Market wants to talk about farewells. No, not here!

Instead, the Italian Market neighbors would rather end this with a salute in not so many words: "Cent' ann'!" which is Italian for, "May you live to be one hundred years!"

RECIPE INDEX

PHOTOGRAPHIC CREDITS

Archdiocesan Archives

The Bulletin

Mario Lanza Institute & Museum

Balch Institute For Ethnic Studies

Free Library of Philadelphia

Temple University Urban Archives

U.S. Department of Justice

Antoinette, Charles Sr. & Charlie Jr. Cannuli, Harry Crimi, DiBruno's, Frank and Roe LaRosa, Michael Malloy, Luke Marano, Sr., Buddy and Aggie Viso.

Memorandum, Coloniale...Vita Coloniale degli Italiani... dal Prof. Alfonso Strafile "Mastro Paolo" Printinghouse, Phila., 1910.

Also: Margaret Jerrido, Brenda Galloway-Wright, Cheryl Johnson, and Sarah Sherman.

ACKNOWLEDGEMENTS

David Auspitz, Victor Baldi, Richard Boardman, Theresa Colaizzo, Vincent Cuffari, Mary Rose Fante Cunningham, Mary & Jack Foti, Joel M. Friedman, Esq., Cathy Gandolfo, Edward Hanlon, Bill and Emilio Mignucci and the DiBruno Girls: Angie, Edith and Rita, Mamma Mia—Ann Morello and Rita Palumbo.

Also: Rita Marsden, Shirley Flaville, the artistically tasteful Frank J. Szerbin, and not least of all, Jack Seidler!

*The author wishes to thank
all of the Italian Market neighbors
for their assistance.*

GENERAL INDEX

NOTES